# TEACHER'S PET PUBLICATIONS

PUZZLE PACK
for
Call It Courage
based on the book by
Armstrong Sperry

Written by
Mary B. Collins

© 2006 Teacher's Pet Publications
All Rights Reserved

The materials in this packet are copyrighted
by Teacher's Pet Publications, Inc.

These pages may be duplicated by the purchaser
for use in the purchaser's own classroom.

Copying any of these materials and distributing them
for any other purpose is a violation of the copyright laws.

© 2006 Teacher's Pet Publications, Inc.
www.tpet.com

INTRODUCTION
If you already own the LitPlan for this title, this Puzzle Pack will refresh your Unit Resource Materials and Vocabulary Resource Materials sections plus give you additional materials you can substitute into the tests. If you do not already have a complete LitPlan, these pages will give you some supplemental materials to use with your own plan. There are two main groups of materials: one set for unit words (such as characters' names, symbols, places, etc.) and one set for vocabulary words associated with the book.

WORD LIST
There is a word list for both the unit words and the vocabulary words. These lists show you which words are being used in the materials and the clues or definitions being used for those words. You may want to give students a word list with clues/definitions to help them, or you may want students to only have a word list (without clues/definitions) if you want them to work a little harder. Both are available for duplication. The word lists can also be your "calling key" for the bingo games.

FILL IN THE BLANK AND MATCHING
There are 4 each of the fill in the blank and matching worksheets for both the unit and vocabulary words. These pages can be used either as extra worksheets for students or as objective parts of a unit test. They can be done individually if students need extra help or as a whole class activity to review the material covered.

MAGIC SQUARES
The magic squares not only reinforce the material covered but also work on reasoning and math skills. Many teachers have told us that their students really enjoy doing these!

WORD SEARCH PUZZLES
The word search words go in all directions, as indicated on your answer keys. Two of the word search puzzles have the clues listed rather than the words. This makes the puzzle a little more difficult, but it reinforces the material better. Two word search puzzles have words only for students who find the clue puzzles too difficult.

CROSSWORD PUZZLES
Both unit and vocabulary word sections have 4 crossword puzzles.

BINGO CARDS
There are 32 individual bingo cards for the unit words and 32 individual bingo cards for the vocabulary words. You can use your word list as a "call list," calling the words at random and marking them off of your list as you go, or you could use the flash cards by cutting them apart and drawing the words at random from a hat (or box or whatever). To make a better review, you might ask for the definition and spelling of each word as you call it out–or you could call out the definitions and have students tell you the words they need to look for on the puzzle.

JUGGLE LETTERS
The vocabulary juggle letter game is intended to help students learn the spellings of the words. One sheet has the definitions listed on it as an extra help for students who need it or to reinforce the definitions if you choose to do so.

FLASH CARDS
We've included a set of vocabulary flash cards you can duplicate, cut, and fold for your students. Some teachers make a few sets for general use by the class; others make a set for each student. Some teachers duplicate them for each student and have the students cut & fold their own. You can cut out just the words and put them in a hat, have each student pick out one word and write the definition and a sentence for that word. Students then swap words and papers, with the next student adding a sentence of his own under the last one. You can have students swap as many times as you like. Each time the student will read the sentences written prior to his own and then add a sentence. You can cut out the words and definitions separately and play "I Have; Who Has?" Each student in the room draws a word and definition. The first student says, "I have (the name of the word). Who has the definition?" The student with the definition reads it then says, "I have (the name of the vocabulary word she has). Who has the definition?" The round continues until all words and definitions have been given.

Call It Courage Word List

No.	Word	Clue/Definition
1.	ARA	Paths of the sea; ocean currents used by Polynesians: ___ Moana
2.	BANANA	This tree's fruit had been cut off recently.
3.	BOAR	Mafatu made a necklace with ____'s teeth.
4.	CANOE	Mafatu built one for his trip home.
5.	COCONUT	Mafatu used its leaves to build a lean-to and drank its juice.
6.	CORAL	It forms the reefs.
7.	COURAGE	Polynesians worshipped it.
8.	DRUMS	The sound of these wakes Mafatu.
9.	EATERS	___-of-men chased Mafatu.
10.	FIFTEEN	Mafatu's age when he went off by himself
11.	FIRE	This at the base of the tree trunk helped Mafatu fell the tree for his canoe.
12.	FISHING	Occupation of the villagers
13.	FORBIDDEN	Where Mafatu landed & eaters-of-men made sacrifices: ___ Island
14.	FOUR	Number of eaters-of-men who chased Mafatu on the island
15.	GHOST	Tupapau or ___ spirit
16.	HEART	Mafatu's christened name: Stout ___
17.	HIKUERU	Island of Mafatu's home
18.	HURRICANE	Killed Mafatu's mother
19.	KANA	Youth who was friendly to Mafatu
20.	KIVI	Deformed albatross & Mafatu's companion
21.	KNIFE	Mafatu made this from whale bone
22.	LAND	Mafatu made new clothing to show he had conquered the ___.
23.	LIME	Mafatu treats his wound with ___ juice.
24.	MAFATU	The Boy Who Was Afraid
25.	MAUI	God of the Fishermen
26.	MOANA	The Sea God
27.	MULBERRY	This tree's bark lining was used to make clothing.
28.	PAREU	Clothing
29.	POLYNESIANS	Native people who lived on the islands
30.	RAFT	Mafatu built one so he could set fish traps.
31.	RUAU	Grandfather who told about the Smoking Islands
32.	SEA	Mafatu feared this.
33.	SHARK	Mafatu killed it by slitting its belly open with his knife.
34.	SMOKING	Home of the eaters-of-men: ___ Island
35.	SPEARHEAD	Mafatu stole it from the statue.
36.	STREAM	Mafatu collapses near one when he arrives at the island.
37.	TAHITI	Island where Mafatu thought he would arrive
38.	TAMANU	Tree used to make the canoe
39.	TAVANA	Chief; Mafatu's father: ___ Nui
40.	TEKOTO	Uninhabited islet where Mafatu and his mother landed
41.	THREE	Mafatu's age when his mother died
42.	URI	Canine companion to Mafatu
43.	WHALE	This skeleton was used for making tools.
44.	YELLOW	Color of Mafatu's dog

Call It Courage Fill In The Blanks 1

_____ 1. Mafatu made this from whale bone

_____ 2. Mafatu built one so he could set fish traps.

_____ 3. Mafatu made new clothing to show he had conquered the ___.

_____ 4. The Sea God

_____ 5. Color of Mafatu's dog

_____ 6. Mafatu's age when his mother died

_____ 7. Uninhabited islet where Mafatu and his mother landed

_____ 8. Mafatu treats his wound with ___ juice.

_____ 9. Mafatu made a necklace with ____'s teeth.

_____ 10. The sound of these wakes Mafatu.

_____ 11. Polynesians worshipped it.

_____ 12. Tree used to make the canoe

_____ 13. Grandfather who told about the Smoking Islands

_____ 14. Killed Mafatu's mother

_____ 15. Number of eaters-of-men who chased Mafatu on the island

_____ 16. The Boy Who Was Afraid

_____ 17. Clothing

_____ 18. ___-of-men chased Mafatu.

_____ 19. This tree's bark lining was used to make clothing.

_____ 20. Mafatu used its leaves to build a lean-to and drank its juice.

Call It Courage Fill In The Blanks 1 Answer Key

KNIFE	1.	Mafatu made this from whale bone
RAFT	2.	Mafatu built one so he could set fish traps.
LAND	3.	Mafatu made new clothing to show he had conquered the ___.
MOANA	4.	The Sea God
YELLOW	5.	Color of Mafatu's dog
THREE	6.	Mafatu's age when his mother died
TEKOTO	7.	Uninhabited islet where Mafatu and his mother landed
LIME	8.	Mafatu treats his wound with ___ juice.
BOAR	9.	Mafatu made a necklace with ____'s teeth.
DRUMS	10.	The sound of these wakes Mafatu.
COURAGE	11.	Polynesians worshipped it.
TAMANU	12.	Tree used to make the canoe
RUAU	13.	Grandfather who told about the Smoking Islands
HURRICANE	14.	Killed Mafatu's mother
FOUR	15.	Number of eaters-of-men who chased Mafatu on the island
MAFATU	16.	The Boy Who Was Afraid
PAREU	17.	Clothing
EATERS	18.	___-of-men chased Mafatu.
MULBERRY	19.	This tree's bark lining was used to make clothing.
COCONUT	20.	Mafatu used its leaves to build a lean-to and drank its juice.

Call It Courage Fill In The Blanks 2

_____ 1. Mafatu used its leaves to build a lean-to and drank its juice.

_____ 2. God of the Fishermen

_____ 3. Home of the eaters-of-men: ___ Island

_____ 4. Where Mafatu landed & eaters-of-men made sacrifices: ___ Island

_____ 5. ___-of-men chased Mafatu.

_____ 6. Uninhabited islet where Mafatu and his mother landed

_____ 7. Grandfather who told about the Smoking Islands

_____ 8. Tree used to make the canoe

_____ 9. Color of Mafatu's dog

_____ 10. The Boy Who Was Afraid

_____ 11. Mafatu's christened name: Stout ___

_____ 12. Mafatu stole it from the statue.

_____ 13. Mafatu made new clothing to show he had conquered the ___.

_____ 14. Mafatu built one so he could set fish traps.

_____ 15. Tupapau or ___ spirit

_____ 16. Mafatu's age when he went off by himself

_____ 17. Island where Mafatu thought he would arrive

_____ 18. Mafatu collapses near one when he arrives at the island.

_____ 19. Deformed albatross & Mafatu's companion

_____ 20. This tree's fruit had been cut off recently.

Call It Courage Fill In The Blanks 2 Answer Key

Answer	Clue
COCONUT	1. Mafatu used its leaves to build a lean-to and drank its juice.
MAUI	2. God of the Fishermen
SMOKING	3. Home of the eaters-of-men: ___ Island
FORBIDDEN	4. Where Mafatu landed & eaters-of-men made sacrifices: ___ Island
EATERS	5. ___-of-men chased Mafatu.
TEKOTO	6. Uninhabited islet where Mafatu and his mother landed
RUAU	7. Grandfather who told about the Smoking Islands
TAMANU	8. Tree used to make the canoe
YELLOW	9. Color of Mafatu's dog
MAFATU	10. The Boy Who Was Afraid
HEART	11. Mafatu's christened name: Stout ___
SPEARHEAD	12. Mafatu stole it from the statue.
LAND	13. Mafatu made new clothing to show he had conquered the ___.
RAFT	14. Mafatu built one so he could set fish traps.
GHOST	15. Tupapau or ___ spirit
FIFTEEN	16. Mafatu's age when he went off by himself
TAHITI	17. Island where Mafatu thought he would arrive
STREAM	18. Mafatu collapses near one when he arrives at the island.
KIVI	19. Deformed albatross & Mafatu's companion
BANANA	20. This tree's fruit had been cut off recently.

Call It Courage Fill In The Blanks 3

_____ 1. The sound of these wakes Mafatu.

_____ 2. Chief; Mafatu's father: ___ Nui

_____ 3. ___-of-men chased Mafatu.

_____ 4. Mafatu killed it by slitting its belly open with his knife.

_____ 5. This skeleton was used for making tools.

_____ 6. Mafatu made a necklace with _____'s teeth.

_____ 7. Island where Mafatu thought he would arrive

_____ 8. Where Mafatu landed & eaters-of-men made sacrifices: ___ Island

_____ 9. God of the Fishermen

_____ 10. Mafatu built one for his trip home.

_____ 11. Occupation of the villagers

_____ 12. Youth who was friendly to Mafatu

_____ 13. Mafatu made new clothing to show he had conquered the ___.

_____ 14. Mafatu used its leaves to build a lean-to and drank its juice.

_____ 15. Mafatu feared this.

_____ 16. Killed Mafatu's mother

_____ 17. Mafatu treats his wound with ___ juice.

_____ 18. Canine companion to Mafatu

_____ 19. Tupapau or ___ spirit

_____ 20. Mafatu's age when his mother died

Call It Courage Fill In The Blanks 3 Answer Key

DRUMS	1. The sound of these wakes Mafatu.
TAVANA	2. Chief; Mafatu's father: ___ Nui
EATERS	3. ___-of-men chased Mafatu.
SHARK	4. Mafatu killed it by slitting its belly open with his knife.
WHALE	5. This skeleton was used for making tools.
BOAR	6. Mafatu made a necklace with ____'s teeth.
TAHITI	7. Island where Mafatu thought he would arrive
FORBIDDEN	8. Where Mafatu landed & eaters-of-men made sacrifices: ___ Island
MAUI	9. God of the Fishermen
CANOE	10. Mafatu built one for his trip home.
FISHING	11. Occupation of the villagers
KANA	12. Youth who was friendly to Mafatu
LAND	13. Mafatu made new clothing to show he had conquered the ___.
COCONUT	14. Mafatu used its leaves to build a lean-to and drank its juice.
SEA	15. Mafatu feared this.
HURRICANE	16. Killed Mafatu's mother
LIME	17. Mafatu treats his wound with ___ juice.
URI	18. Canine companion to Mafatu
GHOST	19. Tupapau or ___ spirit
THREE	20. Mafatu's age when his mother died

Call It Courage Fill In The Blanks 4

_____ 1. Tupapau or ___ spirit

_____ 2. Mafatu built one for his trip home.

_____ 3. Mafatu built one so he could set fish traps.

_____ 4. Canine companion to Mafatu

_____ 5. This skeleton was used for making tools.

_____ 6. Mafatu's age when his mother died

_____ 7. Deformed albatross & Mafatu's companion

_____ 8. Killed Mafatu's mother

_____ 9. Clothing

_____ 10. Mafatu treats his wound with ___ juice.

_____ 11. Mafatu's christened name: Stout ___

_____ 12. ___-of-men chased Mafatu.

_____ 13. Uninhabited islet where Mafatu and his mother landed

_____ 14. Island of Mafatu's home

_____ 15. The sound of these wakes Mafatu.

_____ 16. Mafatu made a necklace with ____'s teeth.

_____ 17. God of the Fishermen

_____ 18. Chief; Mafatu's father: ___ Nui

_____ 19. This tree's bark lining was used to make clothing.

_____ 20. Native people who lived on the islands

Call It Courage Fill In The Blanks 4 Answer Key

GHOST	1. Tupapau or ___ spirit
CANOE	2. Mafatu built one for his trip home.
RAFT	3. Mafatu built one so he could set fish traps.
URI	4. Canine companion to Mafatu
WHALE	5. This skeleton was used for making tools.
THREE	6. Mafatu's age when his mother died
KIVI	7. Deformed albatross & Mafatu's companion
HURRICANE	8. Killed Mafatu's mother
PAREU	9. Clothing
LIME	10. Mafatu treats his wound with ___ juice.
HEART	11. Mafatu's christened name: Stout ___
EATERS	12. ___-of-men chased Mafatu.
TEKOTO	13. Uninhabited islet where Mafatu and his mother landed
HIKUERU	14. Island of Mafatu's home
DRUMS	15. The sound of these wakes Mafatu.
BOAR	16. Mafatu made a necklace with ____'s teeth.
MAUI	17. God of the Fishermen
TAVANA	18. Chief; Mafatu's father: ___ Nui
MULBERRY	19. This tree's bark lining was used to make clothing.
POLYNESIANS	20. Native people who lived on the islands

Call It Courage Matching 1

___ 1. GHOST   A. It forms the reefs.
___ 2. FOUR   B. Home of the eaters-of-men: ___ Island
___ 3. MAFATU   C. Mafatu's age when he went off by himself
___ 4. FORBIDDEN   D. Killed Mafatu's mother
___ 5. FIFTEEN   E. Grandfather who told about the Smoking Islands
___ 6. SPEARHEAD   F. Tupapau or ___ spirit
___ 7. CANOE   G. Mafatu made this from whale bone
___ 8. COCONUT   H. Mafatu stole it from the statue.
___ 9. THREE   I. Mafatu used its leaves to build a lean-to and drank its juice.
___ 10. RAFT   J. Mafatu built one for his trip home.
___ 11. HIKUERU   K. Polynesians worshipped it.
___ 12. SMOKING   L. This skeleton was used for making tools.
___ 13. LAND   M. Number of eaters-of-men who chased Mafatu on the island
___ 14. FISHING   N. Mafatu's age when his mother died
___ 15. TAHITI   O. The Boy Who Was Afraid
___ 16. CORAL   P. ___-of-men chased Mafatu.
___ 17. KIVI   Q. Island of Mafatu's home
___ 18. COURAGE   R. This at the base of the tree trunk helped Mafatu fell the tree for his canoe.
___ 19. KNIFE   S. Mafatu made new clothing to show he had conquered the ___.
___ 20. EATERS   T. Mafatu built one so he could set fish traps.
___ 21. RUAU   U. Occupation of the villagers
___ 22. HURRICANE   V. Deformed albatross & Mafatu's companion
___ 23. FIRE   W. Uninhabited islet where Mafatu and his mother landed
___ 24. WHALE   X. Where Mafatu landed & eaters-of-men made sacrifices: ___ Island
___ 25. TEKOTO   Y. Island where Mafatu thought he would arrive

Call It Courage Matching 1 Answer Key

F - 1.	GHOST	A.	It forms the reefs.
M - 2.	FOUR	B.	Home of the eaters-of-men: ___ Island
O - 3.	MAFATU	C.	Mafatu's age when he went off by himself
X - 4.	FORBIDDEN	D.	Killed Mafatu's mother
C - 5.	FIFTEEN	E.	Grandfather who told about the Smoking Islands
H - 6.	SPEARHEAD	F.	Tupapau or ___ spirit
J - 7.	CANOE	G.	Mafatu made this from whale bone
I - 8.	COCONUT	H.	Mafatu stole it from the statue.
N - 9.	THREE	I.	Mafatu used its leaves to build a lean-to and drank its juice.
T - 10.	RAFT	J.	Mafatu built one for his trip home.
Q - 11.	HIKUERU	K.	Polynesians worshipped it.
B - 12.	SMOKING	L.	This skeleton was used for making tools.
S - 13.	LAND	M.	Number of eaters-of-men who chased Mafatu on the island
U - 14.	FISHING	N.	Mafatu's age when his mother died
Y - 15.	TAHITI	O.	The Boy Who Was Afraid
A - 16.	CORAL	P.	___-of-men chased Mafatu.
V - 17.	KIVI	Q.	Island of Mafatu's home
K - 18.	COURAGE	R.	This at the base of the tree trunk helped Mafatu fell the tree for his canoe.
G - 19.	KNIFE	S.	Mafatu made new clothing to show he had conquered the ___.
P - 20.	EATERS	T.	Mafatu built one so he could set fish traps.
E - 21.	RUAU	U.	Occupation of the villagers
D - 22.	HURRICANE	V.	Deformed albatross & Mafatu's companion
R - 23.	FIRE	W.	Uninhabited islet where Mafatu and his mother landed
L - 24.	WHALE	X.	Where Mafatu landed & eaters-of-men made sacrifices: ___ Island
W - 25.	TEKOTO	Y.	Island where Mafatu thought he would arrive

Call It Courage Matching 2

___ 1. RAFT
___ 2. EATERS
___ 3. FOUR
___ 4. POLYNESIANS
___ 5. FIFTEEN
___ 6. TAHITI
___ 7. THREE
___ 8. STREAM
___ 9. KIVI
___ 10. WHALE
___ 11. URI
___ 12. RUAU
___ 13. HIKUERU
___ 14. COURAGE
___ 15. SHARK
___ 16. TAMANU
___ 17. TEKOTO
___ 18. LAND
___ 19. MULBERRY
___ 20. ARA
___ 21. FIRE
___ 22. BANANA
___ 23. YELLOW
___ 24. BOAR
___ 25. LIME

A. Mafatu built one so he could set fish traps.
B. Canine companion to Mafatu
C. This skeleton was used for making tools.
D. Deformed albatross & Mafatu's companion
E. Mafatu's age when he went off by himself
F. This tree's bark lining was used to make clothing.
G. Color of Mafatu's dog
H. Number of eaters-of-men who chased Mafatu on the island
I. Island of Mafatu's home
J. Mafatu killed it by slitting its belly open with his knife.
K. Mafatu made a necklace with ____'s teeth.
L. Tree used to make the canoe
M. This at the base of the tree trunk helped Mafatu fell the tree for his canoe.
N. Polynesians worshipped it.
O. Uninhabited islet where Mafatu and his mother landed
P. Mafatu's age when his mother died
Q. ___-of-men chased Mafatu.
R. Mafatu treats his wound with ___ juice.
S. This tree's fruit had been cut off recently.
T. Island where Mafatu thought he would arrive
U. Mafatu collapses near one when he arrives at the island.
V. Native people who lived on the islands
W. Paths of the sea; ocean currents used by Polynesians: ___ Moana
X. Grandfather who told about the Smoking Islands
Y. Mafatu made new clothing to show he had conquered the ___.

Call It Courage Matching 2 Answer Key

A - 1. RAFT	A.	Mafatu built one so he could set fish traps.
Q - 2. EATERS	B.	Canine companion to Mafatu
H - 3. FOUR	C.	This skeleton was used for making tools.
V - 4. POLYNESIANS	D.	Deformed albatross & Mafatu's companion
E - 5. FIFTEEN	E.	Mafatu's age when he went off by himself
T - 6. TAHITI	F.	This tree's bark lining was used to make clothing.
P - 7. THREE	G.	Color of Mafatu's dog
U - 8. STREAM	H.	Number of eaters-of-men who chased Mafatu on the island
D - 9. KIVI	I.	Island of Mafatu's home
C - 10. WHALE	J.	Mafatu killed it by slitting its belly open with his knife.
B - 11. URI	K.	Mafatu made a necklace with ____'s teeth.
X - 12. RUAU	L.	Tree used to make the canoe
I - 13. HIKUERU	M.	This at the base of the tree trunk helped Mafatu fell the tree for his canoe.
N - 14. COURAGE	N.	Polynesians worshipped it.
J - 15. SHARK	O.	Uninhabited islet where Mafatu and his mother landed
L - 16. TAMANU	P.	Mafatu's age when his mother died
O - 17. TEKOTO	Q.	___-of-men chased Mafatu.
Y - 18. LAND	R.	Mafatu treats his wound with ___ juice.
F - 19. MULBERRY	S.	This tree's fruit had been cut off recently.
W - 20. ARA	T.	Island where Mafatu thought he would arrive
M - 21. FIRE	U.	Mafatu collapses near one when he arrives at the island.
S - 22. BANANA	V.	Native people who lived on the islands
G - 23. YELLOW	W.	Paths of the sea; ocean currents used by Polynesians: ___ Moana
K - 24. BOAR	X.	Grandfather who told about the Smoking Islands
R - 25. LIME	Y.	Mafatu made new clothing to show he had conquered the ___.

Call It Courage Matching 3

___ 1. CORAL   A. Clothing
___ 2. MAFATU   B. Tree used to make the canoe
___ 3. PAREU   C. This tree's fruit had been cut off recently.
___ 4. HIKUERU   D. Occupation of the villagers
___ 5. FIFTEEN   E. The Boy Who Was Afraid
___ 6. GHOST   F. Mafatu made new clothing to show he had conquered the ___.
___ 7. THREE   G. Native people who lived on the islands
___ 8. DRUMS   H. Mafatu's age when he went off by himself
___ 9. SPEARHEAD   I. It forms the reefs.
___10. FISHING   J. Where Mafatu landed & eaters-of-men made sacrifices: ___ Island
___11. LAND   K. Mafatu made a necklace with ____'s teeth.
___12. KIVI   L. Mafatu killed it by slitting its belly open with his knife.
___13. MAUI   M. Mafatu treats his wound with ___ juice.
___14. TAVANA   N. Mafatu built one for his trip home.
___15. POLYNESIANS   O. Mafatu's age when his mother died
___16. CANOE   P. Mafatu used its leaves to build a lean-to and drank its juice.
___17. LIME   Q. God of the Fishermen
___18. BOAR   R. Island where Mafatu thought he would arrive
___19. RUAU   S. Deformed albatross & Mafatu's companion
___20. BANANA   T. The sound of these wakes Mafatu.
___21. SHARK   U. Island of Mafatu's home
___22. TAMANU   V. Mafatu stole it from the statue.
___23. FORBIDDEN   W. Tupapau or ___ spirit
___24. TAHITI   X. Grandfather who told about the Smoking Islands
___25. COCONUT   Y. Chief; Mafatu's father: ___ Nui

Call It Courage Matching 3 Answer Key

I - 1. CORAL		A. Clothing
E - 2. MAFATU		B. Tree used to make the canoe
A - 3. PAREU		C. This tree's fruit had been cut off recently.
U - 4. HIKUERU		D. Occupation of the villagers
H - 5. FIFTEEN		E. The Boy Who Was Afraid
W - 6. GHOST		F. Mafatu made new clothing to show he had conquered the ___.
O - 7. THREE		G. Native people who lived on the islands
T - 8. DRUMS		H. Mafatu's age when he went off by himself
V - 9. SPEARHEAD		I. It forms the reefs.
D -10. FISHING		J. Where Mafatu landed & eaters-of-men made sacrifices: ___ Island
F -11. LAND		K. Mafatu made a necklace with ____'s teeth.
S -12. KIVI		L. Mafatu killed it by slitting its belly open with his knife.
Q -13. MAUI		M. Mafatu treats his wound with ___ juice.
Y -14. TAVANA		N. Mafatu built one for his trip home.
G -15. POLYNESIANS		O. Mafatu's age when his mother died
N -16. CANOE		P. Mafatu used its leaves to build a lean-to and drank its juice.
M -17. LIME		Q. God of the Fishermen
K -18. BOAR		R. Island where Mafatu thought he would arrive
X -19. RUAU		S. Deformed albatross & Mafatu's companion
C -20. BANANA		T. The sound of these wakes Mafatu.
L -21. SHARK		U. Island of Mafatu's home
B -22. TAMANU		V. Mafatu stole it from the statue.
J -23. FORBIDDEN		W. Tupapau or ___ spirit
R -24. TAHITI		X. Grandfather who told about the Smoking Islands
P -25. COCONUT		Y. Chief; Mafatu's father: ___ Nui

Call It Courage Matching 4

___ 1. WHALE A. Tupapau or ___ spirit
___ 2. SPEARHEAD B. This skeleton was used for making tools.
___ 3. DRUMS C. It forms the reefs.
___ 4. COCONUT D. The Boy Who Was Afraid
___ 5. TAVANA E. Grandfather who told about the Smoking Islands
___ 6. SHARK F. Native people who lived on the islands
___ 7. THREE G. Mafatu's age when his mother died
___ 8. SEA H. This at the base of the tree trunk helped Mafatu fell the tree for his canoe.
___ 9. COURAGE I. ___-of-men chased Mafatu.
___ 10. FIRE J. Mafatu feared this.
___ 11. YELLOW K. Mafatu killed it by slitting its belly open with his knife.
___ 12. TAMANU L. Canine companion to Mafatu
___ 13. CORAL M. Deformed albatross & Mafatu's companion
___ 14. RUAU N. Mafatu stole it from the statue.
___ 15. KNIFE O. Number of eaters-of-men who chased Mafatu on the island
___ 16. FORBIDDEN P. Chief; Mafatu's father: ___ Nui
___ 17. EATERS Q. Mafatu's age when he went off by himself
___ 18. FIFTEEN R. Polynesians worshipped it.
___ 19. FOUR S. Mafatu used its leaves to build a lean-to and drank its juice.
___ 20. MAFATU T. Where Mafatu landed & eaters-of-men made sacrifices: ___ Island
___ 21. KIVI U. Tree used to make the canoe
___ 22. URI V. Occupation of the villagers
___ 23. FISHING W. The sound of these wakes Mafatu.
___ 24. POLYNESIANS X. Color of Mafatu's dog
___ 25. GHOST Y. Mafatu made this from whale bone

Call It Courage Matching 4 Answer Key

B - 1.	WHALE	A. Tupapau or ___ spirit
N - 2.	SPEARHEAD	B. This skeleton was used for making tools.
W - 3.	DRUMS	C. It forms the reefs.
S - 4.	COCONUT	D. The Boy Who Was Afraid
P - 5.	TAVANA	E. Grandfather who told about the Smoking Islands
K - 6.	SHARK	F. Native people who lived on the islands
G - 7.	THREE	G. Mafatu's age when his mother died
J - 8.	SEA	H. This at the base of the tree trunk helped Mafatu fell the tree for his canoe.
R - 9.	COURAGE	I. ___-of-men chased Mafatu.
H - 10.	FIRE	J. Mafatu feared this.
X - 11.	YELLOW	K. Mafatu killed it by slitting its belly open with his knife.
U - 12.	TAMANU	L. Canine companion to Mafatu
C - 13.	CORAL	M. Deformed albatross & Mafatu's companion
E - 14.	RUAU	N. Mafatu stole it from the statue.
Y - 15.	KNIFE	O. Number of eaters-of-men who chased Mafatu on the island
T - 16.	FORBIDDEN	P. Chief; Mafatu's father: ___ Nui
I - 17.	EATERS	Q. Mafatu's age when he went off by himself
Q - 18.	FIFTEEN	R. Polynesians worshipped it.
O - 19.	FOUR	S. Mafatu used its leaves to build a lean-to and drank its juice.
D - 20.	MAFATU	T. Where Mafatu landed & eaters-of-men made sacrifices: ___ Island
M - 21.	KIVI	U. Tree used to make the canoe
L - 22.	URI	V. Occupation of the villagers
V - 23.	FISHING	W. The sound of these wakes Mafatu.
F - 24.	POLYNESIANS	X. Color of Mafatu's dog
A - 25.	GHOST	Y. Mafatu made this from whale bone

Call It Courage Magic Squares 1

Match the definition with the vocabulary word. Put your answers in the magic squares below. When your answers are correct, all columns and rows will add to the same number.

A. COCONUT
B. COURAGE
C. RUAU
D. MOANA
E. FORBIDDEN
F. FIFTEEN
G. HURRICANE
H. SHARK
I. POLYNESIANS
J. LAND
K. MULBERRY
L. KIVI
M. HEART
N. LIME
O. SEA
P. FOUR

1. Mafatu killed it by slitting its belly open with his knife.
2. Mafatu used its leaves to build a lean-to and drank its juice.
3. Polynesians worshipped it.
4. Killed Mafatu's mother
5. Mafatu made new clothing to show he had conquered the ___.
6. Mafatu feared this.
7. Number of eaters-of-men who chased Mafatu on the island
8. Native people who lived on the islands
9. This tree's bark lining was used to make clothing.
10. Mafatu treats his wound with ___ juice.
11. Mafatu's christened name: Stout ___
12. Deformed albatross & Mafatu's companion
13. Where Mafatu landed & eaters-of-men made sacrifices: ___ Island
14. The Sea God
15. Grandfather who told about the Smoking Islands
16. Mafatu's age when he went off by himself

A=	B=	C=	D=
E=	F=	G=	H=
I=	J=	K=	L=
M=	N=	O=	P=

Call It Courage Magic Squares 1 Answer Key

Match the definition with the vocabulary word. Put your answers in the magic squares below. When your answers are correct, all columns and rows will add to the same number.

A. COCONUT   E. FORBIDDEN   I. POLYNESIANS   M. HEART
B. COURAGE   F. FIFTEEN   J. LAND   N. LIME
C. RUAU   G. HURRICANE   K. MULBERRY   O. SEA
D. MOANA   H. SHARK   L. KIVI   P. FOUR

1. Mafatu killed it by slitting its belly open with his knife.
2. Mafatu used its leaves to build a lean-to and drank its juice.
3. Polynesians worshipped it.
4. Killed Mafatu's mother
5. Mafatu made new clothing to show he had conquered the ___.
6. Mafatu feared this.
7. Number of eaters-of-men who chased Mafatu on the island
8. Native people who lived on the islands
9. This tree's bark lining was used to make clothing.
10. Mafatu treats his wound with ___ juice.
11. Mafatu's christened name: Stout ___
12. Deformed albatross & Mafatu's companion
13. Where Mafatu landed & eaters-of-men made sacrifices: ___ Island
14. The Sea God
15. Grandfather who told about the Smoking Islands
16. Mafatu's age when he went off by himself

A=2	B=3	C=15	D=14
E=13	F=16	G=4	H=1
I=8	J=5	K=9	L=12
M=11	N=10	O=6	P=7

Call It Courage Magic Squares 2

Match the definition with the vocabulary word. Put your answers in the magic squares below. When your answers are correct, all columns and rows will add to the same number.

A. BANANA
B. HURRICANE
C. SPEARHEAD
D. COCONUT
E. CANOE
F. TAHITI
G. URI
H. CORAL
I. STREAM
J. PAREU
K. FISHING
L. FIRE
M. SHARK
N. RAFT
O. EATERS
P. TAMANU

1. This tree's fruit had been cut off recently.
2. Mafatu built one so he could set fish traps.
3. Clothing
4. Mafatu built one for his trip home.
5. Canine companion to Mafatu
6. This at the base of the tree trunk helped Mafatu fell the tree for his canoe.
7. Tree used to make the canoe
8. Mafatu stole it from the statue.
9. ___-of-men chased Mafatu.
10. Mafatu used its leaves to build a lean-to and drank its juice.
11. It forms the reefs.
12. Occupation of the villagers
13. Mafatu collapses near one when he arrives at the island.
14. Island where Mafatu thought he would arrive
15. Killed Mafatu's mother
16. Mafatu killed it by slitting its belly open with his knife.

A=	B=	C=	D=
E=	F=	G=	H=
I=	J=	K=	L=
M=	N=	O=	P=

Call It Courage Magic Squares 2 Answer Key

Match the definition with the vocabulary word. Put your answers in the magic squares below. When your answers are correct, all columns and rows will add to the same number.

A. BANANA
B. HURRICANE
C. SPEARHEAD
D. COCONUT
E. CANOE
F. TAHITI
G. URI
H. CORAL
I. STREAM
J. PAREU
K. FISHING
L. FIRE
M. SHARK
N. RAFT
O. EATERS
P. TAMANU

1. This tree's fruit had been cut off recently.
2. Mafatu built one so he could set fish traps.
3. Clothing
4. Mafatu built one for his trip home.
5. Canine companion to Mafatu
6. This at the base of the tree trunk helped Mafatu fell the tree for his canoe.
7. Tree used to make the canoe
8. Mafatu stole it from the statue.
9. ___-of-men chased Mafatu.
10. Mafatu used its leaves to build a lean-to and drank its juice.
11. It forms the reefs.
12. Occupation of the villagers
13. Mafatu collapses near one when he arrives at the island.
14. Island where Mafatu thought he would arrive
15. Killed Mafatu's mother
16. Mafatu killed it by slitting its belly open with his knife.

A=1	B=15	C=8	D=10
E=4	F=14	G=5	H=11
I=13	J=3	K=12	L=6
M=16	N=2	O=9	P=7

Call It Courage Magic Squares 3

Match the definition with the vocabulary word. Put your answers in the magic squares below. When your answers are correct, all columns and rows will add to the same number.

A. PAREU
B. YELLOW
C. RAFT
D. SEA

E. COCONUT
F. TAMANU
G. WHALE
H. FIRE

I. FISHING
J. MAFATU
K. SHARK
L. DRUMS

M. COURAGE
N. HURRICANE
O. FOUR
P. URI

1. Number of eaters-of-men who chased Mafatu on the island
2. The Boy Who Was Afraid
3. This at the base of the tree trunk helped Mafatu fell the tree for his canoe.
4. Clothing
5. Mafatu feared this.
6. Mafatu used its leaves to build a lean-to and drank its juice.
7. Mafatu killed it by slicking its belly open with his knife.
8. Killed Mafatu's mother
9. Tree used to make the canoe
10. Mafatu built one so he could set fish traps.
11. Polynesians worshipped it.
12. The sound of these wakes Mafatu.
13. Occupation of the villagers
14. Canine companion to Mafatu
15. Color of Mafatu's dog
16. This skeleton was used for making tools.

A=	B=	C=	D=
E=	F=	G=	H=
I=	J=	K=	L=
M=	N=	O=	P=

Call It Courage Magic Squares 3 Answer Key

Match the definition with the vocabulary word. Put your answers in the magic squares below. When your answers are correct, all columns and rows will add to the same number.

A. PAREU
B. YELLOW
C. RAFT
D. SEA
E. COCONUT
F. TAMANU
G. WHALE
H. FIRE
I. FISHING
J. MAFATU
K. SHARK
L. DRUMS
M. COURAGE
N. HURRICANE
O. FOUR
P. URI

1. Number of eaters-of-men who chased Mafatu on the island
2. The Boy Who Was Afraid
3. This at the base of the tree trunk helped Mafatu fell the tree for his canoe.
4. Clothing
5. Mafatu feared this.
6. Mafatu used its leaves to build a lean-to and drank its juice.
7. Mafatu killed it by slicking its belly open with his knife.
8. Killed Mafatu's mother
9. Tree used to make the canoe
10. Mafatu built one so he could set fish traps.
11. Polynesians worshipped it.
12. The sound of these wakes Mafatu.
13. Occupation of the villagers
14. Canine companion to Mafatu
15. Color of Mafatu's dog
16. This skeleton was used for making tools.

A=4	B=15	C=10	D=5
E=6	F=9	G=16	H=3
I=13	J=2	K=7	L=12
M=11	N=8	O=1	P=14

Call It Courage Magic Squares 4

Match the definition with the vocabulary word. Put your answers in the magic squares below. When your answers are correct, all columns and rows will add to the same number.

A. HURRICANE   E. GHOST   I. MAFATU   M. BANANA
B. FIRE   F. SMOKING   J. CANOE   N. MAUI
C. MOANA   G. POLYNESIANS   K. COURAGE   O. SHARK
D. BOAR   H. RAFT   L. RUAU   P. THREE

1. The Sea God
2. Mafatu built one for his trip home.
3. Home of the eaters-of-men: ___ Island
4. Mafatu killed it by slicking its belly open with his knife.
5. Mafatu's age when his mother died
6. Tupapau or ___ spirit
7. The Boy Who Was Afraid
8. Mafatu made a necklace with ____'s teeth.
9. This tree's fruit had been cut off recently.
10. Mafatu built one so he could set fish traps.
11. Grandfather who told about the Smoking Islands
12. Killed Mafatu's mother
13. This at the base of the tree trunk helped Mafatu fell the tree for his canoe.
14. Polynesians worshipped it.
15. Native people who lived on the islands
16. God of the Fishermen

A=	B=	C=	D=
E=	F=	G=	H=
I=	J=	K=	L=
M=	N=	O=	P=

27
Copyrighted

Call It Courage Magic Squares 4 Answer Key

Match the definition with the vocabulary word. Put your answers in the magic squares below. When your answers are correct, all columns and rows will add to the same number.

A. HURRICANE   E. GHOST   I. MAFATU   M. BANANA
B. FIRE   F. SMOKING   J. CANOE   N. MAUI
C. MOANA   G. POLYNESIANS K. COURAGE   O. SHARK
D. BOAR   H. RAFT   L. RUAU   P. THREE

1. The Sea God
2. Mafatu built one for his trip home.
3. Home of the eaters-of-men: ___ Island
4. Mafatu killed it by slicking its belly open with his knife.
5. Mafatu's age when his mother died
6. Tupapau or ___ spirit
7. The Boy Who Was Afraid
8. Mafatu made a necklace with ____'s teeth.
9. This tree's fruit had been cut off recently.
10. Mafatu built one so he could set fish traps.
11. Grandfather who told about the Smoking Islands
12. Killed Mafatu's mother
13. This at the base of the tree trunk helped Mafatu fell the tree for his canoe.
14. Polynesians worshipped it.
15. Native people who lived on the islands
16. God of the Fishermen

A=12	B=13	C=1	D=8
E=6	F=3	G=15	H=10
I=7	J=2	K=14	L=11
M=9	N=16	O=4	P=5

Call It Courage Word Search 1

```
G H O S T A M A N U J Y E L L O W H R Q
P O L Y N E S I A N S C I F I S H I N G
P L V S P P K X R X M T O H T F V O K C
D B K R K L K M N V I D J C I M T T X F
X M Z E W L U T Q H C X S S O K R O B K
F T S T T L M F A M P H C P X N U K O F
N P T A B T A T P N A I E E L D U E A Z
T H R E E A E G A R U O C A N O E T R B
L L R T N M R G A A G O N R R N X A W U
R R K A I L T P M M R D F H R T Q V U S
Y J N L V W S S K A E J G E L T H A A F
X A I G B M M V L R G M H A P F U N D R
B X F W O N U X I Z A W S D F R A A Y K
U V E K H K R F I F T E E N V O T R R X
F R I A M A D Z A M Y T A X M F U A H S
G N I N J P L T M W F H K S A F H R H W
G G P A R E U E H T F D D R M S K I V I
```

- Canine companion to Mafatu (3)
- Chief; Mafatu's father: ___ Nui (6)
- Clothing (5)
- Color of Mafatu's dog (6)
- Deformed albatross & Mafatu's companion (4)
- God of the Fishermen (4)
- Grandfather who told about the Smoking Islands (4)
- Home of the eaters-of-men: ___ Island (7)
- Island of Mafatu's home (7)
- Island where Mafatu thought he would arrive (6)
- It forms the reefs. (5)
- Mafatu built one for his trip home. (5)
- Mafatu built one so he could set fish traps. (4)
- Mafatu collapses near one when he arrives at the island. (6)
- Mafatu feared this. (3)
- Mafatu killed it by slitting its belly open with his knife. (5)
- Mafatu made a necklace with ____'s teeth. (4)
- Mafatu made new clothing to show he had conquered the ___. (4)
- Mafatu made this from whale bone (5)
- Mafatu stole it from the statue. (9)
- Mafatu treats his wound with ___ juice. (4)
- Mafatu used its leaves to build a lean-to and drank its juice. (7)
- Mafatu's age when he went off by himself (7)
- Mafatu's age when his mother died (5)
- Mafatu's christened name: Stout ___ (5)
- Native people who lived on the islands (11)
- Number of eaters-of-men who chased Mafatu on the island (4)
- Occupation of the villagers (7)
- Paths of the sea; ocean currents used by Polynesians: ___ Moana (3)
- Polynesians worshipped it. (7)
- The Boy Who Was Afraid (6)
- The Sea God (5)
- The sound of these wakes Mafatu. (5)
- This at the base of the tree trunk helped Mafatu fell the tree for his canoe. (4)
- This skeleton was used for making tools. (5)
- This tree's bark lining was used to make clothing. (8)
- This tree's fruit had been cut off recently. (6)
- Tree used to make the canoe (6)
- Tupapau or ___ spirit (5)
- Uninhabited islet where Mafatu and his mother landed (6)
- Youth who was friendly to Mafatu (4)
- ___-of-men chased Mafatu. (6)

Call It Courage Word Search 1 Answer Key

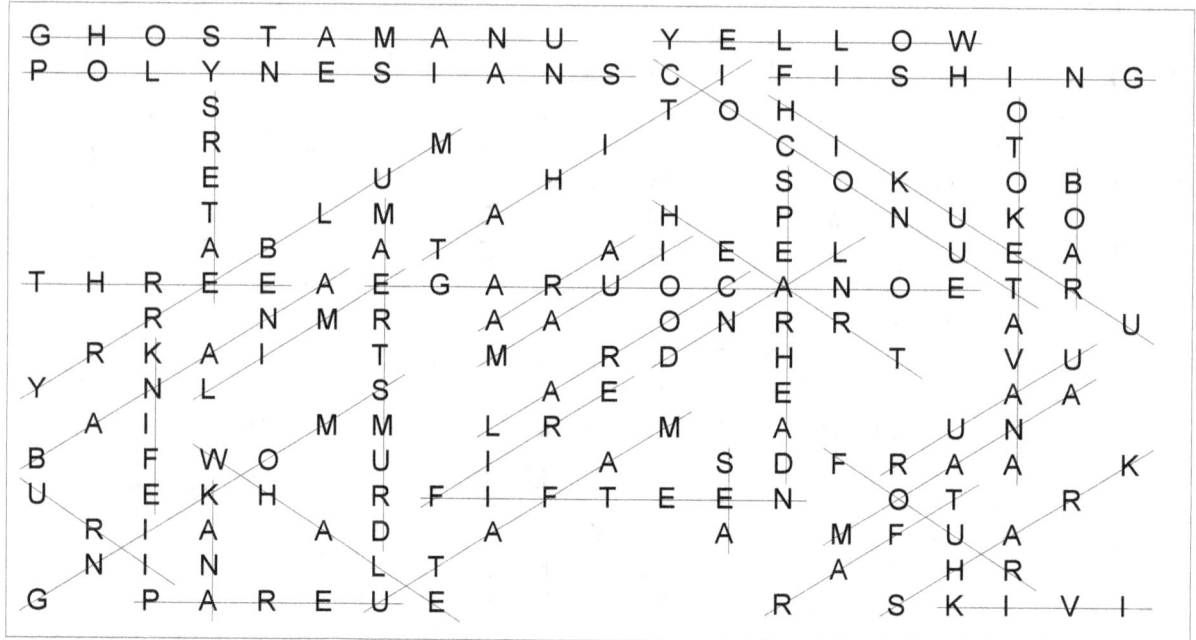

Canine companion to Mafatu (3)
Chief; Mafatu's father: ___ Nui (6)
Clothing (5)
Color of Mafatu's dog (6)
Deformed albatross & Mafatu's companion (4)
God of the Fishermen (4)
Grandfather who told about the Smoking Islands (4)
Home of the eaters-of-men: ___ Island (7)
Island of Mafatu's home (7)
Island where Mafatu thought he would arrive (6)
It forms the reefs. (5)
Mafatu built one for his trip home. (5)
Mafatu built one so he could set fish traps. (4)
Mafatu collapses near one when he arrives at the island. (6)
Mafatu feared this. (3)
Mafatu killed it by slitting its belly open with his knife. (5)
Mafatu made a necklace with ____'s teeth. (4)
Mafatu made new clothing to show he had conquered the ___. (4)
Mafatu made this from whale bone (5)
Mafatu stole it from the statue. (9)
Mafatu treats his wound with ___ juice. (4)
Mafatu used its leaves to build a lean-to and drank its juice. (7)
Mafatu's age when he went off by himself (7)
Mafatu's age when his mother died (5)
Mafatu's christened name: Stout ___ (5)
Native people who lived on the islands (11)
Number of eaters-of-men who chased Mafatu on the island (4)
Occupation of the villagers (7)
Paths of the sea; ocean currents used by Polynesians: ___ Moana (3)
Polynesians worshipped it. (7)
The Boy Who Was Afraid (6)
The Sea God (5)
The sound of these wakes Mafatu. (5)
This at the base of the tree trunk helped Mafatu fell the tree for his canoe. (4)
This skeleton was used for making tools. (5)
This tree's bark lining was used to make clothing. (8)
This tree's fruit had been cut off recently. (6)
Tree used to make the canoe (6)
Tupapau or ___ spirit (5)
Uninhabited islet where Mafatu and his mother landed (6)
Youth who was friendly to Mafatu (4)
___-of-men chased Mafatu. (6)

Call It Courage Word Search 2

```
S T R E A M P C O U R A G E M V A E T M
G X K R N F O Z Y H G N A M O N F F H N
C S A E A I L D C I V R P A I A I R S
M O R B N S Y R F K M C A K N R H F E M
B I R Q A H N U O U M U A K A K E T E R
F W T A B I E M G E K C L N C K A E S Y
B G H A L N S S D R T I O B O N R E H S
J X Z A V G I M Q U V T V C E E T N A C
J H S X L A A G L V O R B I O R Q T R F
T Y J W Q E N G P K V X W Z G N R Y K M
S V R M S A S A E T Z M A F A T U Y Y W
Q S Y Q N T S T M B P C H M G N Q T X Q
F X I R P E A W A Q S W D G A T G X S L
O R Q X G R L H U S G E N M P H B W R W
U E R A P S E M I L N D A G H O S T Q Q
R H Z J M J Q B W T K T L R Q J N X N P
Y E L L O W F O R B I D D E N R U A U X
```

Canine companion to Mafatu (3)
Chief; Mafatu's father: ___ Nui (6)
Clothing (5)
Color of Mafatu's dog (6)
Deformed albatross & Mafatu's companion (4)
God of the Fishermen (4)
Grandfather who told about the Smoking Islands (4)
Home of the eaters-of-men: ___ Island (7)
Island of Mafatu's home (7)
Island where Mafatu thought he would arrive (6)
It forms the reefs. (5)
Mafatu built one for his trip home. (5)
Mafatu built one so he could set fish traps. (4)
Mafatu collapses near one when he arrives at the island. (6)
Mafatu feared this. (3)
Mafatu killed it by slitting its belly open with his knife. (5)
Mafatu made a necklace with ____'s teeth. (4)
Mafatu made new clothing to show he had conquered the ___. (4)
Mafatu made this from whale bone (5)
Mafatu treats his wound with ___ juice. (4)
Mafatu used its leaves to build a lean-to and drank its juice. (7)

Mafatu's age when he went off by himself (7)
Mafatu's age when his mother died (5)
Mafatu's christened name: Stout ___ (5)
Native people who lived on the islands (11)
Number of eaters-of-men who chased Mafatu on the island (4)
Occupation of the villagers (7)
Paths of the sea; ocean currents used by Polynesians: ___ Moana (3)
Polynesians worshipped it. (7)
The Boy Who Was Afraid (6)
The Sea God (5)
The sound of these wakes Mafatu. (5)
This at the base of the tree trunk helped Mafatu fell the tree for his canoe. (4)
This skeleton was used for making tools. (5)
This tree's bark lining was used to make clothing. (8)
This tree's fruit had been cut off recently. (6)
Tree used to make the canoe (6)
Tupapau or ___ spirit (5)
Uninhabited islet where Mafatu and his mother landed (6)
Where Mafatu landed & eaters-of-men made sacrifices: ___ Island (9)
Youth who was friendly to Mafatu (4)
___-of-men chased Mafatu. (6)

Call It Courage Word Search 2 Answer Key

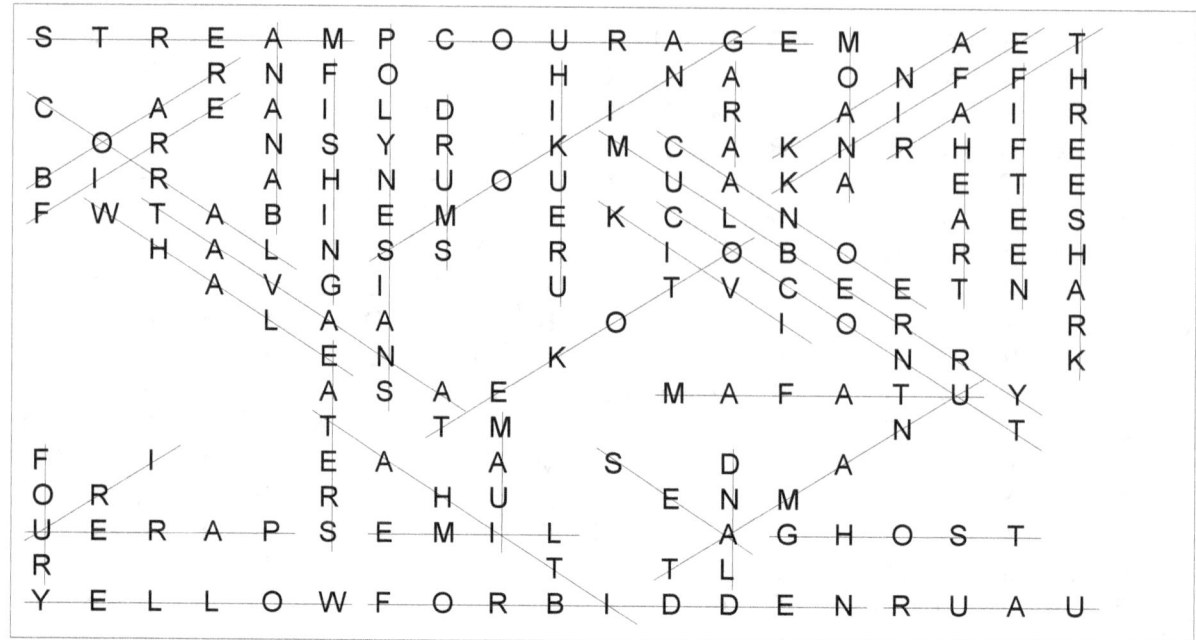

Canine companion to Mafatu (3)
Chief; Mafatu's father: ___ Nui (6)
Clothing (5)
Color of Mafatu's dog (6)
Deformed albatross & Mafatu's companion (4)
God of the Fishermen (4)
Grandfather who told about the Smoking Islands (4)
Home of the eaters-of-men: ___ Island (7)
Island of Mafatu's home (7)
Island where Mafatu thought he would arrive (6)
It forms the reefs. (5)
Mafatu built one for his trip home. (5)
Mafatu built one so he could set fish traps. (4)
Mafatu collapses near one when he arrives at the island. (6)
Mafatu feared this. (3)
Mafatu killed it by slitting its belly open with his knife. (5)
Mafatu made a necklace with ____'s teeth. (4)
Mafatu made new clothing to show he had conquered the ___. (4)
Mafatu made this from whale bone (5)
Mafatu treats his wound with ___ juice. (4)
Mafatu used its leaves to build a lean-to and drank its juice. (7)
Mafatu's age when he went off by himself (7)
Mafatu's age when his mother died (5)
Mafatu's christened name: Stout ___ (5)
Native people who lived on the islands (11)
Number of eaters-of-men who chased Mafatu on the island (4)
Occupation of the villagers (7)
Paths of the sea; ocean currents used by Polynesians: ___ Moana (3)
Polynesians worshipped it. (7)
The Boy Who Was Afraid (6)
The Sea God (5)
The sound of these wakes Mafatu. (5)
This at the base of the tree trunk helped Mafatu fell the tree for his canoe. (4)
This skeleton was used for making tools. (5)
This tree's bark lining was used to make clothing. (8)
This tree's fruit had been cut off recently. (6)
Tree used to make the canoe (6)
Tupapau or ___ spirit (5)
Uninhabited islet where Mafatu and his mother landed (6)
Where Mafatu landed & eaters-of-men made sacrifices: ___ Island (9)
Youth who was friendly to Mafatu (4)
___-of-men chased Mafatu. (6)

Call It Courage Word Search 3

```
B O A R T T D X P H M K T B B H E W Y N
T E W D H M R W Z E A N N A G Q A H X J
L G N G T I U W C A F I F N X H T A S L
T A W N V Z M F Z R A F T A Q Y E L G J
L R X I F L S I I T T E K N F S R E Y Y
M U K K O M H S D F U H N A Q G S N L K
B O G O R K Z H C W T Q W O L L E Y B V
C C T M B W Y I H F B E G M H M S I K W
L W R S I L Y N Y F Q M E H W R T P F V
J F X Z D V J G V K T I L N O I R O Y C
B S K M D H L D Q X J L F R H S T L X J
P Z L F E S W H U R R I C A N E T Y L N
H P V X N S P Y C J D H T R G R V N S M
I D W C H T R E V F Y N C B A F Z E X C
K P G R T R A Q A S F R W Z Z F F S T L
U A F D E E G V C R C O C O N U T I H S
E R D B Z O K O A R H C S S W N R A R Z
R E L W Z N R O R N A E H V T U T N E E
U U N A M A T U T N A M A E R T S S E L
M D A F L C O Q A O X R R D G G T E T H
P Z B U R F Z K K Z A N K M A U I A C G
```

ARA	FIFTEEN	KANA	PAREU	TAHITI
BANANA	FIRE	KIVI	POLYNESIANS	TAMANU
BOAR	FISHING	KNIFE	RAFT	TAVANA
CANOE	FORBIDDEN	LAND	RUAU	TEKOTO
COCONUT	FOUR	LIME	SEA	THREE
CORAL	GHOST	MAFATU	SHARK	URI
COURAGE	HEART	MAUI	SMOKING	WHALE
DRUMS	HIKUERU	MOANA	SPEARHEAD	YELLOW
EATERS	HURRICANE	MULBERRY	STREAM	

Call It Courage Word Search 3 Answer Key

ARA	FIFTEEN	KANA	PAREU	TAHITI
BANANA	FIRE	KIVI	POLYNESIANS	TAMANU
BOAR	FISHING	KNIFE	RAFT	TAVANA
CANOE	FORBIDDEN	LAND	RUAU	TEKOTO
COCONUT	FOUR	LIME	SEA	THREE
CORAL	GHOST	MAFATU	SHARK	URI
COURAGE	HEART	MAUI	SMOKING	WHALE
DRUMS	HIKUERU	MOANA	SPEARHEAD	YELLOW
EATERS	HURRICANE	MULBERRY	STREAM	

Call It Courage Word Search 4

```
C A N O E Y E L L O W T P A R E U S B K
G N Q X X G A J D T A A E N S E F P A K
W A Q K A R B H S V M M R K M R C E N M
H K H R O W M O A N A A R O H O A A M R
R T U C D M H N F G E N F A K T C R N F
W O R V R G A A X N R U T H I Y O H A L
C K R V U J Z L L C T Z T S N J N E H C
Z Z I Y M Q T K I E S M Q W G C U A I P
C K C J S Q P V A D C G L P G B T D K T
N K A V G J I T N Y W L D J J S W Y U H
T M N N P K E Q P N J P T X W F C L E D
S S E K Q R D L O F Y X D B C J M M R P
M R S J S Y P Y L O H R H G F W P Y U V
G C C G Q H K R Y R K W P B Q D P Z D M
P F B H S T M R N B W V T Z B M D T F B
S F I Q J B V E E I P S C P B D S A R L
T J T S X S E B S D H C Q F N J H H G D
G K N U H T T L I D F E V O R L C I T E
F X B R F I L U A E Y X A U A A N T R V
M A U I F G N M N N B O A R E E M I L P
M A F A T U K G S P D U A S T E F I N K
```

ARA	FIFTEEN	KANA	PAREU	TAHITI
BANANA	FIRE	KIVI	POLYNESIANS	TAMANU
BOAR	FISHING	KNIFE	RAFT	TAVANA
CANOE	FORBIDDEN	LAND	RUAU	TEKOTO
COCONUT	FOUR	LIME	SEA	THREE
CORAL	GHOST	MAFATU	SHARK	URI
COURAGE	HEART	MAUI	SMOKING	WHALE
DRUMS	HIKUERU	MOANA	SPEARHEAD	YELLOW
EATERS	HURRICANE	MULBERRY	STREAM	

Call It Courage Word Search 4 Answer Key

ARA	FIFTEEN	KANA	PAREU	TAHITI
BANANA	FIRE	KIVI	POLYNESIANS	TAMANU
BOAR	FISHING	KNIFE	RAFT	TAVANA
CANOE	FORBIDDEN	LAND	RUAU	TEKOTO
COCONUT	FOUR	LIME	SEA	THREE
CORAL	GHOST	MAFATU	SHARK	URI
COURAGE	HEART	MAUI	SMOKING	WHALE
DRUMS	HIKUERU	MOANA	SPEARHEAD	YELLOW
EATERS	HURRICANE	MULBERRY	STREAM	

Call It Courage Crossword 1

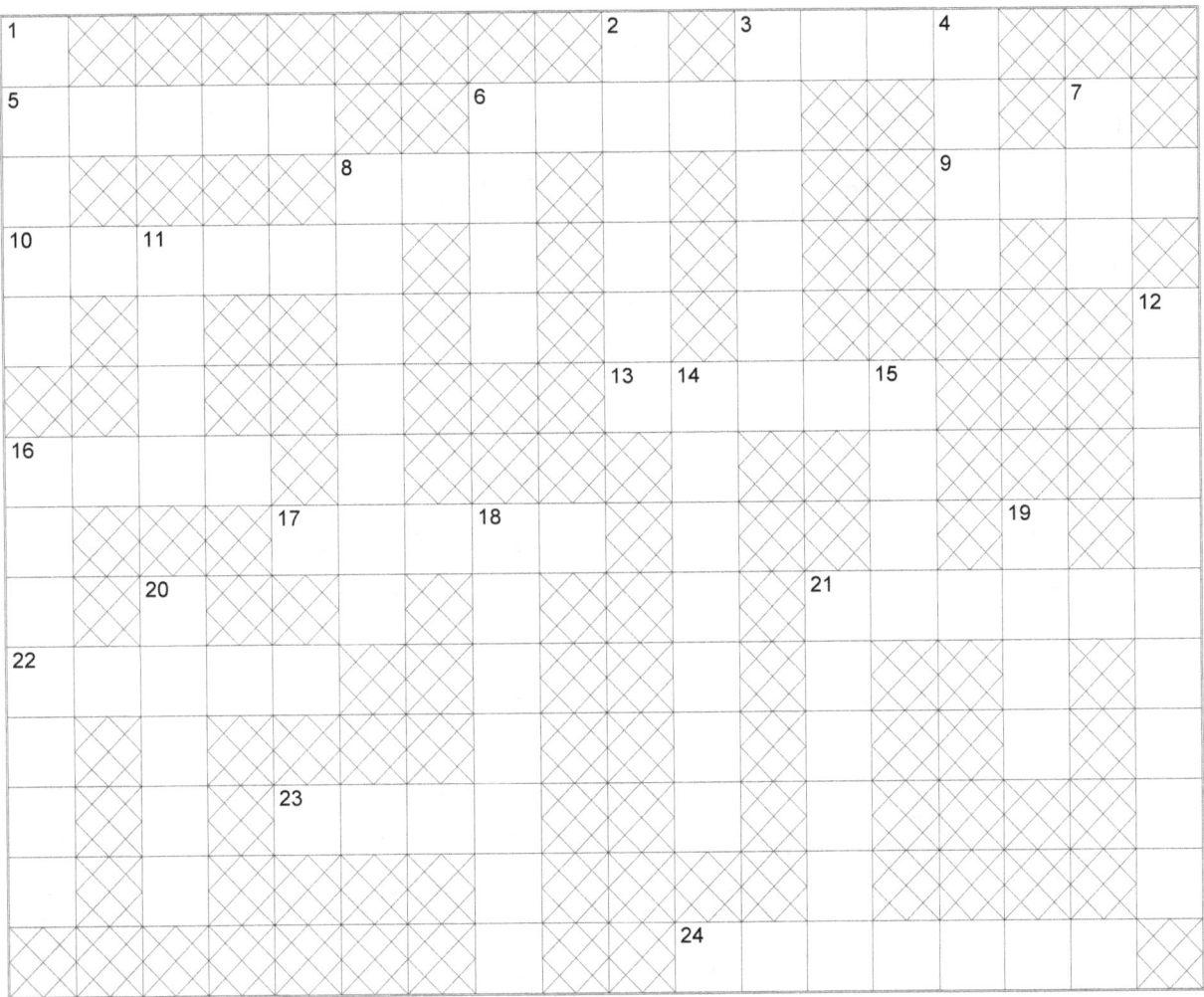

Across
3. Mafatu made a necklace with ____'s teeth.
5. Mafatu's christened name: Stout ___
6. The Sea God
8. Mafatu feared this.
9. This at the base of the tree trunk helped Mafatu fell the tree for his canoe.
10. Mafatu collapses near one when he arrives at the island.
13. Mafatu killed it by slitting its belly open with his knife.
16. Number of eaters-of-men who chased Mafatu on the island
17. Mafatu made this from whale bone
21. Island where Mafatu thought he would arrive
22. Mafatu's age when his mother died
23. Deformed albatross & Mafatu's companion
24. Polynesians worshipped it.

Down
1. Tupapau or ___ spirit
2. ___-of-men chased Mafatu.
3. This tree's fruit had been cut off recently.
4. Mafatu built one so he could set fish traps.
6. God of the Fishermen
7. Canine companion to Mafatu
8. Home of the eaters-of-men: ___ Island
11. Grandfather who told about the Smoking Islands
12. Killed Mafatu's mother
14. Island of Mafatu's home
15. Youth who was friendly to Mafatu
16. Mafatu's age when he went off by himself
18. Occupation of the villagers
19. Mafatu treats his wound with ___ juice.
20. The sound of these wakes Mafatu.
21. Tree used to make the canoe

Call It Courage Crossword 1 Answer Key

	1 G						2 E		3 B	O	A	4 R		
5 H	E	A	R	T		6 M	O	A	N	A		A		7 U
O					8 S	E	A		T			9 F	I	R E
10 S	11 T	R	E	A	M		U		E		A		T	I
T	U				O		I		R		N			12 H
	A				K			13 S	14 H	A	15 R	K		U
16 F	O	U	R		I				I			A		R
I			17 K	N	I	18 F	E		K			N	19 L	R
F		20 D		G		I			U		21 T	A	H I T I
22 T	H	R	E	E		S			E		A		M	C
E		U				H			R		M		E	A
E		M		23 K	I	V	I		U		A			N
N		S				N			N					E
						G		24 C	O	U	R	A	G	E

Across
3. Mafatu made a necklace with ____'s teeth.
5. Mafatu's christened name: Stout ___
6. The Sea God
8. Mafatu feared this.
9. This at the base of the tree trunk helped Mafatu fell the tree for his canoe.
10. Mafatu collapses near one when he arrives at the island.
13. Mafatu killed it by slitting its belly open with his knife.
16. Number of eaters-of-men who chased Mafatu on the island
17. Mafatu made this from whale bone
21. Island where Mafatu thought he would arrive
22. Mafatu's age when his mother died
23. Deformed albatross & Mafatu's companion
24. Polynesians worshipped it.

Down
1. Tupapau or ___ spirit
2. ___-of-men chased Mafatu.
3. This tree's fruit had been cut off recently.
4. Mafatu built one so he could set fish traps.
6. God of the Fishermen
7. Canine companion to Mafatu
8. Home of the eaters-of-men: ___ Island
11. Grandfather who told about the Smoking Islands
12. Killed Mafatu's mother
14. Island of Mafatu's home
15. Youth who was friendly to Mafatu
16. Mafatu's age when he went off by himself
18. Occupation of the villagers
19. Mafatu treats his wound with ___ juice.
20. The sound of these wakes Mafatu.
21. Tree used to make the canoe

Call It Courage Crossword 2

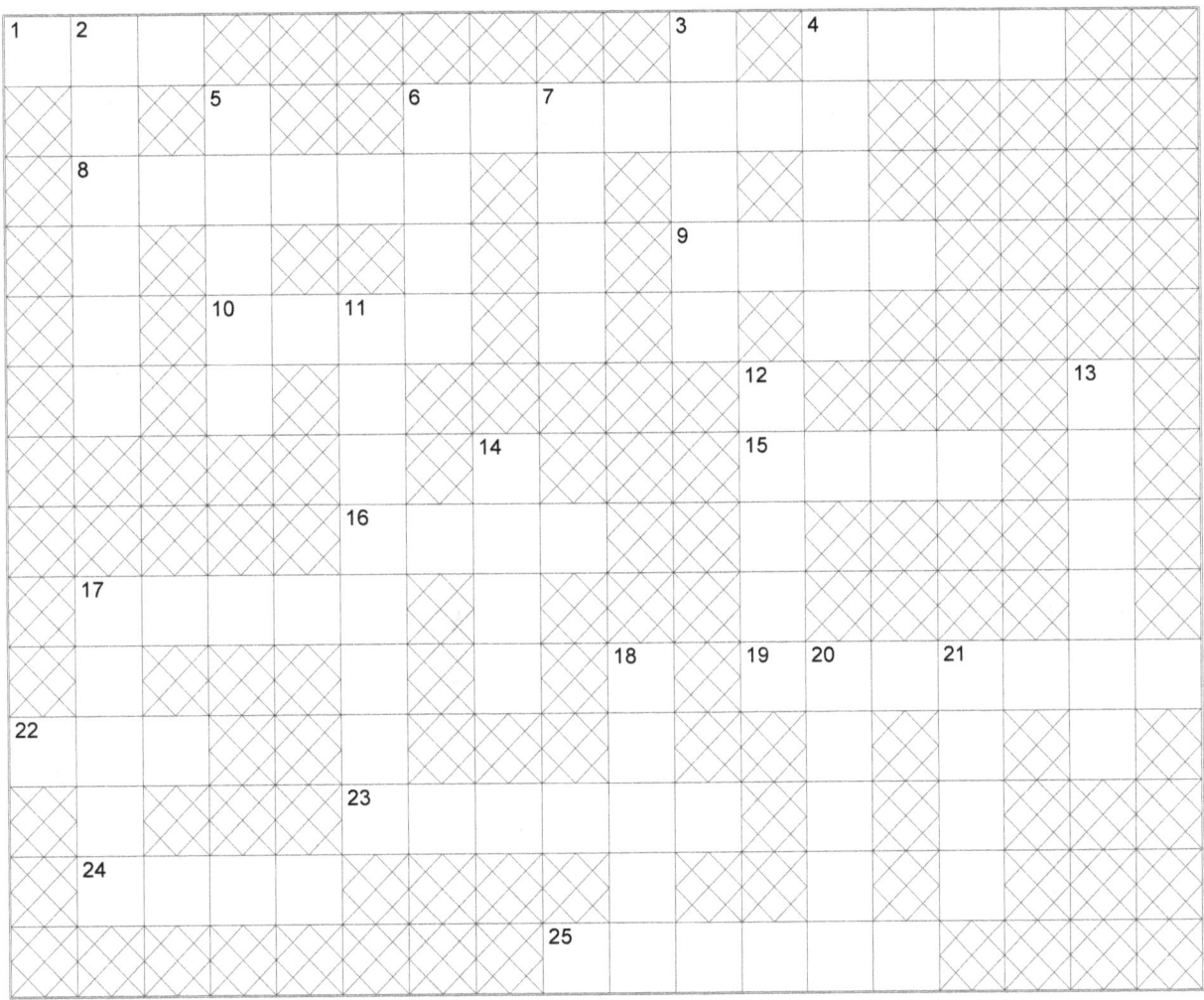

Across
1. Mafatu feared this.
4. Youth who was friendly to Mafatu
6. Mafatu's age when he went off by himself
8. Island where Mafatu thought he would arrive
9. Mafatu built one so he could set fish traps.
10. Mafatu treats his wound with ___ juice.
15. Grandfather who told about the Smoking Islands
16. Mafatu made a necklace with ____'s teeth.
17. Mafatu built one for his trip home.
19. Home of the eaters-of-men: ___ Island
22. Canine companion to Mafatu
23. Color of Mafatu's dog
24. Mafatu made new clothing to show he had conquered the ___.
25. Mafatu collapses near one when he arrives at the island.

Down
2. ___-of-men chased Mafatu.
3. Mafatu's christened name: Stout ___
4. Mafatu made this from whale bone
5. This skeleton was used for making tools.
6. This at the base of the tree trunk helped Mafatu fell the tree for his canoe.
7. Number of eaters-of-men who chased Mafatu on the island
11. This tree's bark lining was used to make clothing.
12. The sound of these wakes Mafatu.
13. This tree's fruit had been cut off recently.
14. God of the Fishermen
17. It forms the reefs.
18. Tupapau or ___ spirit
20. The Sea God
21. Deformed albatross & Mafatu's companion

Call It Courage Crossword 2 Answer Key

	1 S	2 E	A						3 H		4 K	A	N	A
		A		5 W		6 F	I	7 F	T	E	E	N		
		8 T	A	H	I	T	I	O		A		I		
		E		A		R	U	9 R	A	F	T			
		R		10 L	11 I	M	E	R		T	E			
		S		E	U					12 D			13 B	
					L	14 M			15 R	U	A	U	A	
				16 B	O	A	R			U			N	
		17 C	A	N	O	E				M			A	
		O			R	I		18 G	19 S	M	20 O	21 K	I	N G
22 U	R	I		R				H		O		I	A	
		A		23 Y	E	L	L	O	W		A		V	
		24 L	A	N	D			S		N		I		
					25 S	T	R	E	A	M				

Across
1. Mafatu feared this.
4. Youth who was friendly to Mafatu
6. Mafatu's age when he went off by himself
8. Island where Mafatu thought he would arrive
9. Mafatu built one so he could set fish traps.
10. Mafatu treats his wound with ___ juice.
15. Grandfather who told about the Smoking Islands
16. Mafatu made a necklace with ____'s teeth.
17. Mafatu built one for his trip home.
19. Home of the eaters-of-men: ___ Island
22. Canine companion to Mafatu
23. Color of Mafatu's dog
24. Mafatu made new clothing to show he had conquered the ___.
25. Mafatu collapses near one when he arrives at the island.

Down
2. ___-of-men chased Mafatu.
3. Mafatu's christened name: Stout ___
4. Mafatu made this from whale bone
5. This skeleton was used for making tools.
6. This at the base of the tree trunk helped Mafatu fell the tree for his canoe.
7. Number of eaters-of-men who chased Mafatu on the island
11. This tree's bark lining was used to make clothing.
12. The sound of these wakes Mafatu.
13. This tree's fruit had been cut off recently.
14. God of the Fishermen
17. It forms the reefs.
18. Tupapau or ___ spirit
20. The Sea God
21. Deformed albatross & Mafatu's companion

Call It Courage Crossword 3

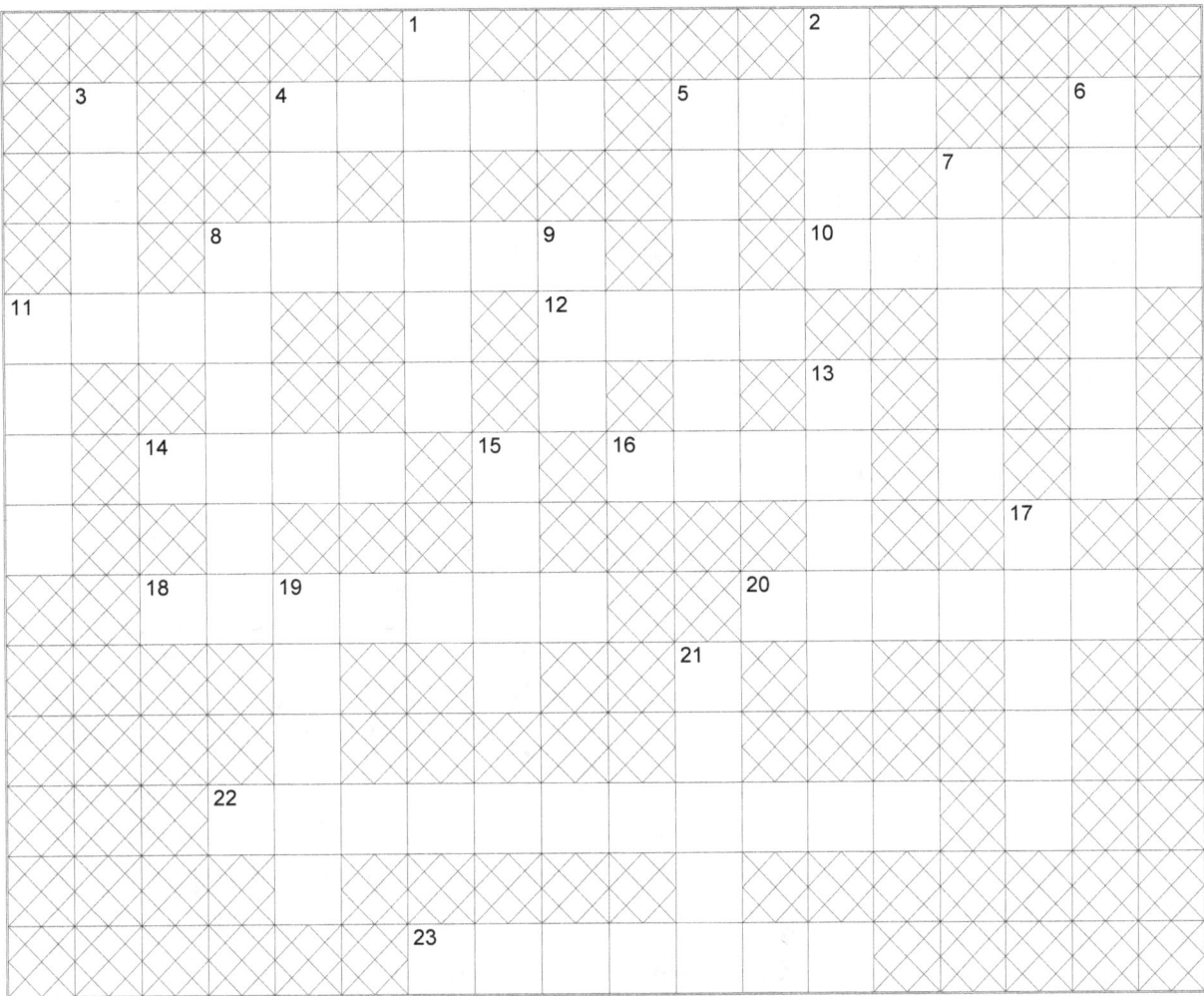

Across
4. Mafatu killed it by slitting its belly open with his knife.
5. Mafatu made a necklace with ____'s teeth.
8. Tree used to make the canoe
10. Island where Mafatu thought he would arrive
11. Mafatu treats his wound with ___ juice.
12. Grandfather who told about the Smoking Islands
14. Number of eaters-of-men who chased Mafatu on the island
16. Youth who was friendly to Mafatu
18. Mafatu used its leaves to build a lean-to and drank its juice.
20. Color of Mafatu's dog
22. Native people who lived on the islands
23. Island of Mafatu's home

Down
1. The Boy Who Was Afraid
2. Mafatu built one so he could set fish traps.
3. Deformed albatross & Mafatu's companion
4. Mafatu feared this.
5. This tree's fruit had been cut off recently.
6. ___-of-men chased Mafatu.
7. Tupapau or ___ spirit
8. Uninhabited islet where Mafatu and his mother landed
9. Canine companion to Mafatu
11. Mafatu made new clothing to show he had conquered the ___.
13. Clothing
15. God of the Fishermen
17. The Sea God
19. Mafatu built one for his trip home.
21. Mafatu made this from whale bone

Call It Courage Crossword 3 Answer Key

			1 M					2 R		
	3 K		4 S	H	A	R	K	5 B	O	A	R	6 E
	I		E		F			A		F	7 G	A
	V		8 T	A	M	A	N	9 U		10 T	A	H	I	T	I
11 L	I	M	E			T		12 R	U	A	U		O	E
A			K			U		I		N	13 P	S	R
N		14 F	O	U	R		15 M	16 K	A	N	A	T	S
D		T					A			R		17 M
		18 C	19 C	O	N	U	T		20 Y	E	L	L	O	W
			A			I		21 K	U		A
			N					N		N
		22 P	O	L	Y	N	E	S	I	A	N	S	A
			E					F
			23 H	I	K	U	E	R	U

Across
4. Mafatu killed it by slitting its belly open with his knife.
5. Mafatu made a necklace with ____'s teeth.
8. Tree used to make the canoe
10. Island where Mafatu thought he would arrive
11. Mafatu treats his wound with ___ juice.
12. Grandfather who told about the Smoking Islands
14. Number of eaters-of-men who chased Mafatu on the island
16. Youth who was friendly to Mafatu
18. Mafatu used its leaves to build a lean-to and drank its juice.
20. Color of Mafatu's dog
22. Native people who lived on the islands
23. Island of Mafatu's home

Down
1. The Boy Who Was Afraid
2. Mafatu built one so he could set fish traps.
3. Deformed albatross & Mafatu's companion
4. Mafatu feared this.
5. This tree's fruit had been cut off recently.
6. ___-of-men chased Mafatu.
7. Tupapau or ___ spirit
8. Uninhabited islet where Mafatu and his mother landed
9. Canine companion to Mafatu
11. Mafatu made new clothing to show he had conquered the ___.
13. Clothing
15. God of the Fishermen
17. The Sea God
19. Mafatu built one for his trip home.
21. Mafatu made this from whale bone

Call It Courage Crossword 4

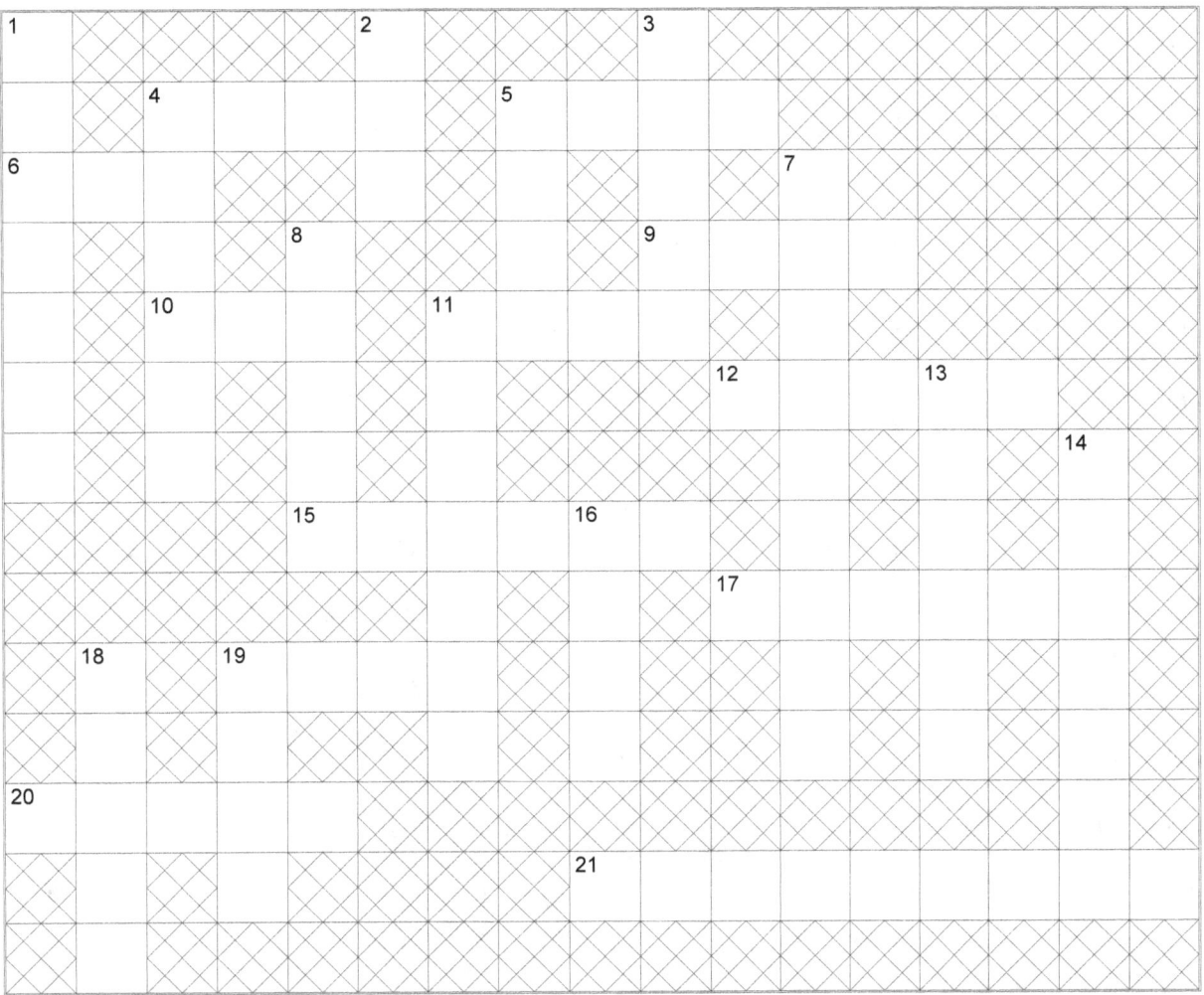

Across
4. Mafatu made a necklace with ____'s teeth.
5. Youth who was friendly to Mafatu
6. Mafatu feared this.
9. Number of eaters-of-men who chased Mafatu on the island
10. Paths of the sea; ocean currents used by Polynesians: ___ Moana
11. This at the base of the tree trunk helped Mafatu fell the tree for his canoe.
12. The sound of these wakes Mafatu.
15. ___-of-men chased Mafatu.
17. Tree used to make the canoe
19. Mafatu treats his wound with ___ juice.
20. The Sea God
21. Where Mafatu landed & eaters-of-men made sacrifices: ___ Island

Down
1. Occupation of the villagers
2. Canine companion to Mafatu
3. Mafatu made this from whale bone
4. This tree's fruit had been cut off recently.
5. Deformed albatross & Mafatu's companion
7. Killed Mafatu's mother
8. Mafatu built one for his trip home.
11. Mafatu's age when he went off by himself
13. The Boy Who Was Afraid
14. Polynesians worshipped it.
16. Mafatu built one so he could set fish traps.
18. Tupapau or ___ spirit
19. Mafatu made new clothing to show he had conquered the ___.

Call It Courage Crossword 4 Answer Key

	1	2	3							
	F		U		K					
	I	4 B	O	A	R	5 K	A	N	A	
6 S	E	A		I		I		I	7 H	
	H		N	8 C		V		9 F	O	U	R
	I	10 A	R	A	11 F	I	R	E	R	
	N	N	N	I			12 D	R	U	13 M	S
	G	A	O	F				I		A	14 C
		15 E	A	T	E	16 R	S		C		F	O
				E		A		17 T	A	M	A	N	U
	18 G	19 L	I	M	E	F			N		T		R
	H	A		N		T			E		U		A
20 M	O	A	N	A								G
	S		D			21 F	O	R	B	I	D	D	E	N
	T												

Across

4. Mafatu made a necklace with ____'s teeth.
5. Youth who was friendly to Mafatu
6. Mafatu feared this.
9. Number of eaters-of-men who chased Mafatu on the island
10. Paths of the sea; ocean currents used by Polynesians: ___ Moana
11. This at the base of the tree trunk helped Mafatu fell the tree for his canoe.
12. The sound of these wakes Mafatu.
15. ___-of-men chased Mafatu.
17. Tree used to make the canoe
19. Mafatu treats his wound with ___ juice.
20. The Sea God
21. Where Mafatu landed & eaters-of-men made sacrifices: ___ Island

Down

1. Occupation of the villagers
2. Canine companion to Mafatu
3. Mafatu made this from whale bone
4. This tree's fruit had been cut off recently.
5. Deformed albatross & Mafatu's companion
7. Killed Mafatu's mother
8. Mafatu built one for his trip home.
11. Mafatu's age when he went off by himself
13. The Boy Who Was Afraid
14. Polynesians worshipped it.
16. Mafatu built one so he could set fish traps.
18. Tupapau or ___ spirit
19. Mafatu made new clothing to show he had conquered the ___.

Call It Courage

TAVANA	LAND	KANA	SHARK	RUAU
RAFT	GHOST	FOUR	HIKUERU	SEA
KIVI	LIME	FREE SPACE	COCONUT	HEART
MAUI	BANANA	ARA	YELLOW	URI
SPEARHEAD	HURRICANE	SMOKING	DRUMS	FIFTEEN

Call It Courage

POLYNESIANS	EATERS	TAMANU	THREE	FORBIDDEN
KNIFE	COURAGE	BOAR	FIRE	STREAM
TEKOTO	PAREU	FREE SPACE	TAHITI	WHALE
CORAL	CANOE	FISHING	MOANA	FIFTEEN
DRUMS	SMOKING	HURRICANE	SPEARHEAD	URI

Call It Courage

SPEARHEAD	LAND	FOUR	SHARK	COURAGE
FIRE	HEART	CORAL	BOAR	URI
SMOKING	TAVANA	FREE SPACE	TEKOTO	ARA
PAREU	STREAM	KIVI	FISHING	EATERS
MULBERRY	FIFTEEN	WHALE	DRUMS	RAFT

Call It Courage

GHOST	TAMANU	MAUI	LIME	THREE
HURRICANE	KANA	KNIFE	FORBIDDEN	HIKUERU
YELLOW	MAFATU	FREE SPACE	CANOE	MOANA
POLYNESIANS	RUAU	SEA	TAHITI	RAFT
DRUMS	WHALE	FIFTEEN	MULBERRY	EATERS

Call It Courage

SHARK	MOANA	POLYNESIANS	GHOST	KANA
MAUI	FISHING	YELLOW	WHALE	CANOE
MULBERRY	HEART	FREE SPACE	TAVANA	TAHITI
FORBIDDEN	FOUR	SEA	TAMANU	BOAR
TEKOTO	PAREU	SPEARHEAD	HIKUERU	CORAL

Call It Courage

LIME	DRUMS	KIVI	COCONUT	EATERS
URI	BANANA	THREE	FIRE	HURRICANE
LAND	RUAU	FREE SPACE	RAFT	COURAGE
KNIFE	FIFTEEN	MAFATU	STREAM	CORAL
HIKUERU	SPEARHEAD	PAREU	TEKOTO	BOAR

Call It Courage

FORBIDDEN	YELLOW	COURAGE	DRUMS	LIME
SHARK	SMOKING	SEA	CANOE	TAHITI
KNIFE	TAMANU	FREE SPACE	MOANA	THREE
MAUI	BOAR	COCONUT	ARA	FIFTEEN
HEART	FIRE	HURRICANE	FISHING	FOUR

Call It Courage

LAND	MULBERRY	TEKOTO	HIKUERU	RAFT
PAREU	RUAU	WHALE	KANA	URI
MAFATU	GHOST	FREE SPACE	KIVI	BANANA
EATERS	SPEARHEAD	CORAL	TAVANA	FOUR
FISHING	HURRICANE	FIRE	HEART	FIFTEEN

Call It Courage

URI	KIVI	SHARK	HIKUERU	THREE
HURRICANE	PAREU	TEKOTO	FORBIDDEN	FIRE
DRUMS	STREAM	FREE SPACE	WHALE	YELLOW
KNIFE	SPEARHEAD	CORAL	GHOST	RAFT
LAND	RUAU	SEA	TAVANA	FIFTEEN

Call It Courage

CANOE	FOUR	POLYNESIANS	EATERS	MOANA
BANANA	LIME	MULBERRY	SMOKING	KANA
BOAR	COCONUT	FREE SPACE	MAUI	TAHITI
HEART	COURAGE	TAMANU	FISHING	FIFTEEN
TAVANA	SEA	RUAU	LAND	RAFT

Call It Courage

POLYNESIANS	FOUR	FORBIDDEN	MAFATU	CANOE
SMOKING	WHALE	RAFT	LAND	LIME
SHARK	HEART	FREE SPACE	TAHITI	KNIFE
MULBERRY	THREE	GHOST	MAUI	COURAGE
FISHING	TAMANU	COCONUT	EATERS	ARA

Call It Courage

RUAU	CORAL	HURRICANE	FIFTEEN	BANANA
SPEARHEAD	DRUMS	YELLOW	HIKUERU	TEKOTO
KANA	SEA	FREE SPACE	PAREU	URI
BOAR	MOANA	TAVANA	STREAM	ARA
EATERS	COCONUT	TAMANU	FISHING	COURAGE

Call It Courage

KNIFE	TEKOTO	GHOST	LIME	BANANA
RAFT	FORBIDDEN	YELLOW	TAHITI	FOUR
FIFTEEN	MAUI	FREE SPACE	KIVI	HIKUERU
LAND	DRUMS	MOANA	COURAGE	SHARK
HURRICANE	MULBERRY	THREE	SEA	HEART

Call It Courage

RUAU	POLYNESIANS	MAFATU	ARA	URI
FISHING	TAMANU	WHALE	COCONUT	SPEARHEAD
STREAM	TAVANA	FREE SPACE	KANA	PAREU
EATERS	BOAR	CORAL	FIRE	HEART
SEA	THREE	MULBERRY	HURRICANE	SHARK

Call It Courage

FOUR	THREE	SMOKING	PAREU	KNIFE
MOANA	EATERS	POLYNESIANS	MULBERRY	KIVI
FISHING	CANOE	FREE SPACE	YELLOW	HURRICANE
ARA	SEA	DRUMS	BANANA	RAFT
COCONUT	TAHITI	FIFTEEN	TEKOTO	MAUI

Call It Courage

URI	WHALE	HEART	SPEARHEAD	LAND
KANA	HIKUERU	COURAGE	MAFATU	GHOST
SHARK	TAVANA	FREE SPACE	TAMANU	BOAR
RUAU	LIME	STREAM	CORAL	MAUI
TEKOTO	FIFTEEN	TAHITI	COCONUT	RAFT

Call It Courage

THREE	FORBIDDEN	WHALE	BANANA	MULBERRY
FIRE	DRUMS	TAMANU	CANOE	LIME
KANA	FISHING	FREE SPACE	FOUR	YELLOW
HURRICANE	KNIFE	CORAL	ARA	STREAM
RAFT	LAND	PAREU	TEKOTO	TAVANA

Call It Courage

HIKUERU	URI	MOANA	BOAR	MAFATU
SPEARHEAD	EATERS	COCONUT	RUAU	KIVI
GHOST	POLYNESIANS	FREE SPACE	SEA	TAHITI
SHARK	FIFTEEN	HEART	SMOKING	TAVANA
TEKOTO	PAREU	LAND	RAFT	STREAM

Call It Courage

MOANA	COURAGE	TAVANA	WHALE	MAFATU
COCONUT	SMOKING	STREAM	MAUI	SPEARHEAD
ARA	THREE	FREE SPACE	TAMANU	POLYNESIANS
KNIFE	FORBIDDEN	SEA	BOAR	TEKOTO
MULBERRY	PAREU	HIKUERU	CORAL	LAND

Call It Courage

EATERS	SHARK	YELLOW	FOUR	FIRE
KIVI	URI	GHOST	RUAU	DRUMS
HURRICANE	FIFTEEN	FREE SPACE	TAHITI	CANOE
KANA	LIME	FISHING	RAFT	LAND
CORAL	HIKUERU	PAREU	MULBERRY	TEKOTO

Call It Courage

URI	HURRICANE	TAVANA	GHOST	HIKUERU
CANOE	MAUI	KNIFE	DRUMS	FISHING
KANA	COURAGE	FREE SPACE	WHALE	POLYNESIANS
BANANA	SPEARHEAD	MAFATU	MOANA	STREAM
SEA	PAREU	TEKOTO	RAFT	LAND

Call It Courage

SHARK	HEART	BOAR	FOUR	TAHITI
THREE	MULBERRY	YELLOW	FIRE	FIFTEEN
TAMANU	FORBIDDEN	FREE SPACE	ARA	EATERS
SMOKING	COCONUT	CORAL	RUAU	LAND
RAFT	TEKOTO	PAREU	SEA	STREAM

Call It Courage

BANANA	BOAR	KNIFE	KIVI	SPEARHEAD
MULBERRY	HURRICANE	COURAGE	GHOST	MAFATU
TAHITI	FOUR	FREE SPACE	POLYNESIANS	FISHING
TEKOTO	FIRE	FIFTEEN	YELLOW	HEART
TAVANA	URI	CANOE	LAND	TAMANU

Call It Courage

HIKUERU	WHALE	PAREU	STREAM	SHARK
SEA	THREE	COCONUT	LIME	ARA
MAUI	EATERS	FREE SPACE	KANA	SMOKING
CORAL	MOANA	FORBIDDEN	RAFT	TAMANU
LAND	CANOE	URI	TAVANA	HEART

Call It Courage

HURRICANE	COURAGE	MULBERRY	COCONUT	SEA
TAHITI	WHALE	FOUR	LAND	CANOE
KNIFE	PAREU	FREE SPACE	HEART	FIRE
FORBIDDEN	BOAR	SMOKING	LIME	ARA
RAFT	DRUMS	CORAL	TEKOTO	HIKUERU

Call It Courage

FISHING	POLYNESIANS	BANANA	MAFATU	THREE
MAUI	FIFTEEN	SPEARHEAD	KIVI	EATERS
MOANA	URI	FREE SPACE	RUAU	STREAM
YELLOW	SHARK	TAVANA	GHOST	HIKUERU
TEKOTO	CORAL	DRUMS	RAFT	ARA

Call It Courage

DRUMS	WHALE	KIVI	HIKUERU	MULBERRY
THREE	EATERS	LIME	MAFATU	BANANA
ARA	POLYNESIANS	FREE SPACE	SHARK	FORBIDDEN
FIRE	TAMANU	TEKOTO	HURRICANE	MAUI
MOANA	KANA	KNIFE	URI	SMOKING

Call It Courage

RAFT	LAND	CORAL	CANOE	SEA
PAREU	FISHING	TAHITI	RUAU	COURAGE
COCONUT	YELLOW	FREE SPACE	BOAR	SPEARHEAD
TAVANA	FOUR	GHOST	STREAM	SMOKING
URI	KNIFE	KANA	MOANA	MAUI

Call It Courage

POLYNESIANS	THREE	KIVI	FORBIDDEN	TAHITI
FOUR	TAMANU	HIKUERU	BOAR	EATERS
CANOE	LIME	FREE SPACE	COURAGE	KANA
FIFTEEN	HURRICANE	YELLOW	WHALE	FISHING
TAVANA	DRUMS	HEART	FIRE	RUAU

Call It Courage

BANANA	LAND	RAFT	TEKOTO	SHARK
MULBERRY	MAUI	SEA	KNIFE	STREAM
URI	MOANA	FREE SPACE	GHOST	ARA
CORAL	PAREU	SMOKING	SPEARHEAD	RUAU
FIRE	HEART	DRUMS	TAVANA	FISHING

Call It Courage

BANANA	FIRE	FISHING	TAMANU	MULBERRY
RAFT	HURRICANE	FIFTEEN	DRUMS	URI
STREAM	SEA	FREE SPACE	KNIFE	SPEARHEAD
MAFATU	LIME	ARA	CANOE	KIVI
HIKUERU	GHOST	LAND	RUAU	SMOKING

Call It Courage

MAUI	COURAGE	BOAR	FORBIDDEN	WHALE
KANA	YELLOW	SHARK	MOANA	THREE
POLYNESIANS	PAREU	FREE SPACE	TEKOTO	HEART
TAHITI	COCONUT	TAVANA	EATERS	SMOKING
RUAU	LAND	GHOST	HIKUERU	KIVI

Call It Courage Vocabulary Word List

No.	Word	Clue/Definition
1.	ADZE	Tool for cutting heavy pieces of wood
2.	APPREHENSION	Worry; nervousness
3.	BOLSTER	Strengthen by encouraging
4.	CAPSIZED	Overturned; caused a boat to overturn
5.	CAUTERIZE	Seal a wound with something that burns
6.	CAUTION	Care; close attention
7.	CONGEALED	Became thick or solid
8.	CONVULSIVELY	In a violently jerking or shaking manner
9.	CULPRIT	Someone who is responsible for a misdeed
10.	DESPAIRING	Feeling hopeless
11.	DIMINISHING	Becoming smaller
12.	DISMAL	Depressing
13.	DISMAY	Feeling of hopelessness or disappointment
14.	ELATION	Feeling of extraordinary happiness and excitement
15.	EXERTION	Physical effort
16.	FELL	Cut down
17.	FIERCE	Ferocious; violent
18.	GRACILE	Gracefully slender
19.	GROTESQUE	Bizarre; gross
20.	IMPENDING	About to happen
21.	IMPETUS	Forward motion; movement
22.	IMPOTENT	Without strength
23.	INDIFFERENCE	Lack of interest or concern
24.	INEVITABLE	Impossible to prevent from happening
25.	INTERVALS	Distances between things
26.	IRRESOLUTE	Unsure; not able to make decisions
27.	JEERED	Mocked by shouting or laughing
28.	LASH	Tie something to another object
29.	LIVID	Very angry
30.	LUMINOUS	Giving off or reflecting light
31.	LURED	Tempted someone to go somewhere
32.	MISSIONARIES	People sent by a church to spread its faith
33.	MUTTER	Complain quietly or indistinctly
34.	OPPRESSIVE	Harsh
35.	PERIL	Danger
36.	PINNACLE	Top; highest point
37.	POISED	Balanced; suspended
38.	PROFANED	Showed disrespect for gods or a religion
39.	PROSTRATE	Lie flat
40.	QUAILING	Trembling or shrinking back with fear
41.	RAMPARTS	Walls of a fort
42.	RELISHING	Taking great pleasure in
43.	RENDING	Tearing apart violently
44.	RUDE	Rough; incomplete
45.	SCORN	Contempt; disrespect
46.	SEIZE	Take hold of quickly and firmly
47.	SIPHONED	Transferred liquid through a tube
48.	STOUT	Brave; sturdy
49.	SULTRY	Very hot and damp
50.	TANTALIZING	Tempting but unavailable
51.	TAUT	Stiff; stretched tight

Call It Courage Vocabulary Word List Continued

No.	Word	Clue/Definition
52.	TUMULT	Noisy uproar
53.	VANTAGE	Position that gives an advantage
54.	VERITABLE	Real; true
55.	WANED	Decreased; got smaller
56.	WARILY	Cautiously
57.	WAXED	Increased; enlarged
58.	WROUGHT	Formed; created

Call It Courage Vocabulary Fill In The Blanks 1

_____ 1. Stiff; stretched tight

_____ 2. Brave; sturdy

_____ 3. Very hot and damp

_____ 4. Feeling hopeless

_____ 5. Becoming smaller

_____ 6. Contempt; disrespect

_____ 7. Cut down

_____ 8. Gracefully slender

_____ 9. Feeling of hopelessness or disappointment

_____ 10. Trembling or shrinking back with fear

_____ 11. Taking great pleasure in

_____ 12. Decreased; got smaller

_____ 13. Complain quietly or indistinctly

_____ 14. Tempted someone to go somewhere

_____ 15. Walls of a fort

_____ 16. Lie flat

_____ 17. Bizarre; gross

_____ 18. Distances between things

_____ 19. Tool for cutting heavy pieces of wood

_____ 20. Without strength

Call It Courage Vocabulary Fill In The Blanks 1 Answer Key

TAUT	1. Stiff; stretched tight
STOUT	2. Brave; sturdy
SULTRY	3. Very hot and damp
DESPAIRING	4. Feeling hopeless
DIMINISHING	5. Becoming smaller
SCORN	6. Contempt; disrespect
FELL	7. Cut down
GRACILE	8. Gracefully slender
DISMAY	9. Feeling of hopelessness or disappointment
QUAILING	10. Trembling or shrinking back with fear
RELISHING	11. Taking great pleasure in
WANED	12. Decreased; got smaller
MUTTER	13. Complain quietly or indistinctly
LURED	14. Tempted someone to go somewhere
RAMPARTS	15. Walls of a fort
PROSTRATE	16. Lie flat
GROTESQUE	17. Bizarre; gross
INTERVALS	18. Distances between things
ADZE	19. Tool for cutting heavy pieces of wood
IMPOTENT	20. Without strength

Call It Courage Vocabulary Fill In The Blanks 2

_____ 1. In a violently jerking or shaking manner

_____ 2. Worry; nervousness

_____ 3. Forward motion; movement

_____ 4. Feeling of hopelessness or disappointment

_____ 5. Danger

_____ 6. Without strength

_____ 7. Depressing

_____ 8. Cautiously

_____ 9. Balanced; suspended

_____ 10. Tempting but unavailable

_____ 11. Brave; sturdy

_____ 12. Strengthen by encouraging

_____ 13. Lack of interest or concern

_____ 14. Ferocious; violent

_____ 15. Taking great pleasure in

_____ 16. Increased; enlarged

_____ 17. Walls of a fort

_____ 18. Noisy uproar

_____ 19. Harsh

_____ 20. Tie something to another object

Call It Courage Vocabulary Fill In The Blanks 2 Answer Key

CONVULSIVELY	1. In a violently jerking or shaking manner
APPREHENSION	2. Worry; nervousness
IMPETUS	3. Forward motion; movement
DISMAY	4. Feeling of hopelessness or disappointment
PERIL	5. Danger
IMPOTENT	6. Without strength
DISMAL	7. Depressing
WARILY	8. Cautiously
POISED	9. Balanced; suspended
TANTALIZING	10. Tempting but unavailable
STOUT	11. Brave; sturdy
BOLSTER	12. Strengthen by encouraging
INDIFFERENCE	13. Lack of interest or concern
FIERCE	14. Ferocious; violent
RELISHING	15. Taking great pleasure in
WAXED	16. Increased; enlarged
RAMPARTS	17. Walls of a fort
TUMULT	18. Noisy uproar
OPPRESSIVE	19. Harsh
LASH	20. Tie something to another object

Call It Courage Vocabulary Fill In The Blanks 3

1. Very angry
2. About to happen
3. Strengthen by encouraging
4. Real; true
5. Feeling hopeless
6. Without strength
7. Seal a wound with something that burns
8. Care; close attention
9. Harsh
10. Walls of a fort
11. Take hold of quickly and firmly
12. Depressing
13. Lie flat
14. Overturned; caused a boat to overturn
15. Position that gives an advantage
16. Distances between things
17. Trembling or shrinking back with fear
18. Complain quietly or indistinctly
19. Contempt; disrespect
20. Mocked by shouting or laughing

Call It Courage Vocabulary Fill In The Blanks 3 Answer Key

LIVID	1. Very angry
IMPENDING	2. About to happen
BOLSTER	3. Strengthen by encouraging
VERITABLE	4. Real; true
DESPAIRING	5. Feeling hopeless
IMPOTENT	6. Without strength
CAUTERIZE	7. Seal a wound with something that burns
CAUTION	8. Care; close attention
OPPRESSIVE	9. Harsh
RAMPARTS	10. Walls of a fort
SEIZE	11. Take hold of quickly and firmly
DISMAL	12. Depressing
PROSTRATE	13. Lie flat
CAPSIZED	14. Overturned; caused a boat to overturn
VANTAGE	15. Position that gives an advantage
INTERVALS	16. Distances between things
QUAILING	17. Trembling or shrinking back with fear
MUTTER	18. Complain quietly or indistinctly
SCORN	19. Contempt; disrespect
JEERED	20. Mocked by shouting or laughing

Call It Courage Vocabulary Fill In The Blanks 4

_____ 1. Bizarre; gross

_____ 2. People sent by a church to spread its faith

_____ 3. Decreased; got smaller

_____ 4. Someone who is responsible for a misdeed

_____ 5. Worry; nervousness

_____ 6. Became thick or solid

_____ 7. Impossible to prevent from happening

_____ 8. Position that gives an advantage

_____ 9. Complain quietly or indistinctly

_____ 10. Cut down

_____ 11. Cautiously

_____ 12. Lie flat

_____ 13. Top; highest point

_____ 14. Formed; created

_____ 15. Contempt; disrespect

_____ 16. Very hot and damp

_____ 17. Feeling of extraordinary happiness and excitement

_____ 18. Showed disrespect for gods or a religion

_____ 19. Transferred liquid through a tube

_____ 20. Balanced; suspended

Call It Courage Vocabulary Fill In The Blanks 4 Answer Key

GROTESQUE	1. Bizarre; gross
MISSIONARIES	2. People sent by a church to spread its faith
WANED	3. Decreased; got smaller
CULPRIT	4. Someone who is responsible for a misdeed
APPREHENSION	5. Worry; nervousness
CONGEALED	6. Became thick or solid
INEVITABLE	7. Impossible to prevent from happening
VANTAGE	8. Position that gives an advantage
MUTTER	9. Complain quietly or indistinctly
FELL	10. Cut down
WARILY	11. Cautiously
PROSTRATE	12. Lie flat
PINNACLE	13. Top; highest point
WROUGHT	14. Formed; created
SCORN	15. Contempt; disrespect
SULTRY	16. Very hot and damp
ELATION	17. Feeling of extraordinary happiness and excitement
PROFANED	18. Showed disrespect for gods or a religion
SIPHONED	19. Transferred liquid through a tube
POISED	20. Balanced; suspended

Call It Courage Vocabulary Matching 1

___ 1. RENDING A. Take hold of quickly and firmly
___ 2. CONGEALED B. Tie something to another object
___ 3. DISMAL C. Stiff; stretched tight
___ 4. CAUTION D. Without strength
___ 5. TAUT E. Contempt; disrespect
___ 6. IMPETUS F. Formed; created
___ 7. QUAILING G. Care; close attention
___ 8. INDIFFERENCE H. Trembling or shrinking back with fear
___ 9. PINNACLE I. Transferred liquid through a tube
___ 10. VANTAGE J. Tearing apart violently
___ 11. GROTESQUE K. Bizarre; gross
___ 12. MISSIONARIES L. Overturned; caused a boat to overturn
___ 13. CAPSIZED M. Gracefully slender
___ 14. GRACILE N. Forward motion; movement
___ 15. IMPOTENT O. Showed disrespect for gods or a religion
___ 16. WROUGHT P. Someone who is responsible for a misdeed
___ 17. FIERCE Q. Position that gives an advantage
___ 18. WAXED R. Became thick or solid
___ 19. SCORN S. Increased; enlarged
___ 20. SIPHONED T. Lack of interest or concern
___ 21. CULPRIT U. Ferocious; violent
___ 22. SEIZE V. Depressing
___ 23. LASH W. Top; highest point
___ 24. PROFANED X. People sent by a church to spread its faith
___ 25. INTERVALS Y. Distances between things

Call It Courage Vocabulary Matching 1 Answer Key

J - 1. RENDING	A. Take hold of quickly and firmly
R - 2. CONGEALED	B. Tie something to another object
V - 3. DISMAL	C. Stiff; stretched tight
G - 4. CAUTION	D. Without strength
C - 5. TAUT	E. Contempt; disrespect
N - 6. IMPETUS	F. Formed; created
H - 7. QUAILING	G. Care; close attention
T - 8. INDIFFERENCE	H. Trembling or shrinking back with fear
W - 9. PINNACLE	I. Transferred liquid through a tube
Q - 10. VANTAGE	J. Tearing apart violently
K - 11. GROTESQUE	K. Bizarre; gross
X - 12. MISSIONARIES	L. Overturned; caused a boat to overturn
L - 13. CAPSIZED	M. Gracefully slender
M - 14. GRACILE	N. Forward motion; movement
D - 15. IMPOTENT	O. Showed disrespect for gods or a religion
F - 16. WROUGHT	P. Someone who is responsible for a misdeed
U - 17. FIERCE	Q. Position that gives an advantage
S - 18. WAXED	R. Became thick or solid
E - 19. SCORN	S. Increased; enlarged
I - 20. SIPHONED	T. Lack of interest or concern
P - 21. CULPRIT	U. Ferocious; violent
A - 22. SEIZE	V. Depressing
B - 23. LASH	W. Top; highest point
O - 24. PROFANED	X. People sent by a church to spread its faith
Y - 25. INTERVALS	Y. Distances between things

Call It Courage Vocabulary Matching 2

___ 1. WROUGHT   A. Tempted someone to go somewhere
___ 2. QUAILING   B. Without strength
___ 3. MUTTER   C. Increased; enlarged
___ 4. SULTRY   D. Walls of a fort
___ 5. IMPETUS   E. Care; close attention
___ 6. SEIZE   F. Stiff; stretched tight
___ 7. EXERTION   G. Trembling or shrinking back with fear
___ 8. SIPHONED   H. Very angry
___ 9. INTERVALS   I. Bizarre; gross
___10. GROTESQUE   J. Cut down
___11. DESPAIRING   K. Feeling hopeless
___12. CONVULSIVELY   L. Formed; created
___13. CAUTION   M. Rough; incomplete
___14. STOUT   N. Real; true
___15. VERITABLE   O. Physical effort
___16. RUDE   P. Transferred liquid through a tube
___17. LIVID   Q. Noisy uproar
___18. TAUT   R. Forward motion; movement
___19. WAXED   S. In a violently jerking or shaking manner
___20. IMPOTENT   T. Very hot and damp
___21. LURED   U. Take hold of quickly and firmly
___22. MISSIONARIES   V. Complain quietly or indistinctly
___23. TUMULT   W. Brave; sturdy
___24. RAMPARTS   X. People sent by a church to spread its faith
___25. FELL   Y. Distances between things

Call It Courage Vocabulary Matching 2 Answer Key

L - 1. WROUGHT		A. Tempted someone to go somewhere
G - 2. QUAILING		B. Without strength
V - 3. MUTTER		C. Increased; enlarged
T - 4. SULTRY		D. Walls of a fort
R - 5. IMPETUS		E. Care; close attention
U - 6. SEIZE		F. Stiff; stretched tight
O - 7. EXERTION		G. Trembling or shrinking back with fear
P - 8. SIPHONED		H. Very angry
Y - 9. INTERVALS		I. Bizarre; gross
I - 10. GROTESQUE		J. Cut down
K - 11. DESPAIRING		K. Feeling hopeless
S - 12. CONVULSIVELY		L. Formed; created
E - 13. CAUTION		M. Rough; incomplete
W - 14. STOUT		N. Real; true
N - 15. VERITABLE		O. Physical effort
M - 16. RUDE		P. Transferred liquid through a tube
H - 17. LIVID		Q. Noisy uproar
F - 18. TAUT		R. Forward motion; movement
C - 19. WAXED		S. In a violently jerking or shaking manner
B - 20. IMPOTENT		T. Very hot and damp
A - 21. LURED		U. Take hold of quickly and firmly
X - 22. MISSIONARIES		V. Complain quietly or indistinctly
Q - 23. TUMULT		W. Brave; sturdy
D - 24. RAMPARTS		X. People sent by a church to spread its faith
J - 25. FELL		Y. Distances between things

Call It Courage Vocabulary Matching 3

___ 1. PROSTRATE   A. Walls of a fort
___ 2. TANTALIZING   B. Rough; incomplete
___ 3. IMPETUS   C. Showed disrespect for gods or a religion
___ 4. RAMPARTS   D. Formed; created
___ 5. VERITABLE   E. Real; true
___ 6. PROFANED   F. Gracefully slender
___ 7. DIMINISHING   G. Noisy uproar
___ 8. IMPENDING   H. Position that gives an advantage
___ 9. LIVID   I. About to happen
___ 10. CAPSIZED   J. Cut down
___ 11. PINNACLE   K. In a violently jerking or shaking manner
___ 12. CONVULSIVELY   L. Very angry
___ 13. GRACILE   M. Becoming smaller
___ 14. VANTAGE   N. Balanced; suspended
___ 15. FELL   O. Lie flat
___ 16. PERIL   P. Forward motion; movement
___ 17. JEERED   Q. Overturned; caused a boat to overturn
___ 18. RENDING   R. Contempt; disrespect
___ 19. RUDE   S. Mocked by shouting or laughing
___ 20. SCORN   T. Danger
___ 21. POISED   U. Top; highest point
___ 22. LUMINOUS   V. Feeling hopeless
___ 23. WROUGHT   W. Tearing apart violently
___ 24. TUMULT   X. Giving off or reflecting light
___ 25. DESPAIRING   Y. Tempting but unavailable

Call It Courage Vocabulary Matching 3 Answer Key

O - 1. PROSTRATE   A. Walls of a fort
Y - 2. TANTALIZING   B. Rough; incomplete
P - 3. IMPETUS   C. Showed disrespect for gods or a religion
A - 4. RAMPARTS   D. Formed; created
E - 5. VERITABLE   E. Real; true
C - 6. PROFANED   F. Gracefully slender
M - 7. DIMINISHING   G. Noisy uproar
I - 8. IMPENDING   H. Position that gives an advantage
L - 9. LIVID   I. About to happen
Q -10. CAPSIZED   J. Cut down
U -11. PINNACLE   K. In a violently jerking or shaking manner
K -12. CONVULSIVELY   L. Very angry
F -13. GRACILE   M. Becoming smaller
H -14. VANTAGE   N. Balanced; suspended
J -15. FELL   O. Lie flat
T -16. PERIL   P. Forward motion; movement
S -17. JEERED   Q. Overturned; caused a boat to overturn
W -18. RENDING   R. Contempt; disrespect
B -19. RUDE   S. Mocked by shouting or laughing
R -20. SCORN   T. Danger
N -21. POISED   U. Top; highest point
X -22. LUMINOUS   V. Feeling hopeless
D -23. WROUGHT   W. Tearing apart violently
G -24. TUMULT   X. Giving off or reflecting light
V -25. DESPAIRING   Y. Tempting but unavailable

Call It Courage Vocabulary Matching 4

___ 1. POISED   A. Balanced; suspended
___ 2. VERITABLE   B. Lie flat
___ 3. IMPENDING   C. Feeling hopeless
___ 4. DESPAIRING   D. Feeling of hopelessness or disappointment
___ 5. CAUTION   E. Someone who is responsible for a misdeed
___ 6. INDIFFERENCE   F. About to happen
___ 7. CONVULSIVELY   G. Complain quietly or indistinctly
___ 8. QUAILING   H. In a violently jerking or shaking manner
___ 9. PROSTRATE   I. Increased; enlarged
___10. WAXED   J. Lack of interest or concern
___11. MISSIONARIES   K. Became thick or solid
___12. CULPRIT   L. Trembling or shrinking back with fear
___13. CAPSIZED   M. Overturned; caused a boat to overturn
___14. WANED   N. Care; close attention
___15. IRRESOLUTE   O. Tool for cutting heavy pieces of wood
___16. ADZE   P. Unsure; not able to make decisions
___17. OPPRESSIVE   Q. Harsh
___18. CONGEALED   R. People sent by a church to spread its faith
___19. VANTAGE   S. Walls of a fort
___20. DISMAL   T. Real; true
___21. DISMAY   U. Showed disrespect for gods or a religion
___22. MUTTER   V. Depressing
___23. RAMPARTS   W. Position that gives an advantage
___24. LURED   X. Decreased; got smaller
___25. PROFANED   Y. Tempted someone to go somewhere

Call It Courage Vocabulary Matching 4 Answer Key

A - 1. POISED	A.	Balanced; suspended
T - 2. VERITABLE	B.	Lie flat
F - 3. IMPENDING	C.	Feeling hopeless
C - 4. DESPAIRING	D.	Feeling of hopelessness or disappointment
N - 5. CAUTION	E.	Someone who is responsible for a misdeed
J - 6. INDIFFERENCE	F.	About to happen
H - 7. CONVULSIVELY	G.	Complain quietly or indistinctly
L - 8. QUAILING	H.	In a violently jerking or shaking manner
B - 9. PROSTRATE	I.	Increased; enlarged
I - 10. WAXED	J.	Lack of interest or concern
R - 11. MISSIONARIES	K.	Became thick or solid
E - 12. CULPRIT	L.	Trembling or shrinking back with fear
M - 13. CAPSIZED	M.	Overturned; caused a boat to overturn
X - 14. WANED	N.	Care; close attention
P - 15. IRRESOLUTE	O.	Tool for cutting heavy pieces of wood
O - 16. ADZE	P.	Unsure; not able to make decisions
Q - 17. OPPRESSIVE	Q.	Harsh
K - 18. CONGEALED	R.	People sent by a church to spread its faith
W - 19. VANTAGE	S.	Walls of a fort
V - 20. DISMAL	T.	Real; true
D - 21. DISMAY	U.	Showed disrespect for gods or a religion
G - 22. MUTTER	V.	Depressing
S - 23. RAMPARTS	W.	Position that gives an advantage
Y - 24. LURED	X.	Decreased; got smaller
U - 25. PROFANED	Y.	Tempted someone to go somewhere

Call It Courage Vocabulary Magic Squares 1

Match the definition with the vocabulary word. Put your answers in the magic squares below. When your answers are correct, all columns and rows will add to the same number.

A. PINNACLE
B. DISMAY
C. LASH
D. MUTTER
E. IRRESOLUTE
F. RUDE
G. IMPOTENT
H. APPREHENSION
I. CULPRIT
J. WARILY
K. SEIZE
L. WAXED
M. POISED
N. TAUT
O. VANTAGE
P. IMPENDING

1. Worry; nervousness
2. Balanced; suspended
3. Feeling of hopelessness or disappointment
4. Take hold of quickly and firmly
5. Cautiously
6. Tie something to another object
7. About to happen
8. Unsure; not able to make decisions
9. Position that gives an advantage
10. Rough; incomplete
11. Someone who is responsible for a misdeed
12. Complain quietly or indistinctly
13. Top; highest point
14. Increased; enlarged
15. Without strength
16. Stiff; stretched tight

A=	B=	C=	D=
E=	F=	G=	H=
I=	J=	K=	L=
M=	N=	O=	P=

Call It Courage Vocabulary Magic Squares 1 Answer Key

Match the definition with the vocabulary word. Put your answers in the magic squares below. When your answers are correct, all columns and rows will add to the same number.

A. PINNACLE
B. DISMAY
C. LASH
D. MUTTER
E. IRRESOLUTE
F. RUDE
G. IMPOTENT
H. APPREHENSION
I. CULPRIT
J. WARILY
K. SEIZE
L. WAXED
M. POISED
N. TAUT
O. VANTAGE
P. IMPENDING

1. Worry; nervousness
2. Balanced; suspended
3. Feeling of hopelessness or disappointment
4. Take hold of quickly and firmly
5. Cautiously
6. Tie something to another object
7. About to happen
8. Unsure; not able to make decisions
9. Position that gives an advantage
10. Rough; incomplete
11. Someone who is responsible for a misdeed
12. Complain quietly or indistinctly
13. Top; highest point
14. Increased; enlarged
15. Without strength
16. Stiff; stretched tight

A=13	B=3	C=6	D=12
E=8	F=10	G=15	H=1
I=11	J=5	K=4	L=14
M=2	N=16	O=9	P=7

Call It Courage Vocabulary Magic Squares 2

Match the definition with the vocabulary word. Put your answers in the magic squares below. When your answers are correct, all columns and rows will add to the same number.

A. TAUT
B. IMPENDING
C. DESPAIRING
D. DIMINISHING
E. DISMAY
F. DISMAL
G. CAPSIZED
H. GRACILE
I. PINNACLE
J. OPPRESSIVE
K. LIVID
L. CONGEALED
M. WROUGHT
N. ADZE
O. ELATION
P. INEVITABLE

1. Depressing
2. Top; highest point
3. Feeling of extraordinary happiness and excitement
4. Becoming smaller
5. Formed; created
6. About to happen
7. Gracefully slender
8. Very angry
9. Feeling hopeless
10. Impossible to prevent from happening
11. Harsh
12. Feeling of hopelessness or disappointment
13. Became thick or solid
14. Overturned; caused a boat to overturn
15. Stiff; stretched tight
16. Tool for cutting heavy pieces of wood

A=	B=	C=	D=
E=	F=	G=	H=
I=	J=	K=	L=
M=	N=	O=	P=

Call It Courage Vocabulary Magic Squares 2 Answer Key

Match the definition with the vocabulary word. Put your answers in the magic squares below. When your answers are correct, all columns and rows will add to the same number.

A. TAUT
B. IMPENDING
C. DESPAIRING
D. DIMINISHING
E. DISMAY
F. DISMAL
G. CAPSIZED
H. GRACILE
I. PINNACLE
J. OPPRESSIVE
K. LIVID
L. CONGEALED
M. WROUGHT
N. ADZE
O. ELATION
P. INEVITABLE

1. Depressing
2. Top; highest point
3. Feeling of extraordinary happiness and excitement
4. Becoming smaller
5. Formed; created
6. About to happen
7. Gracefully slender
8. Very angry
9. Feeling hopeless
10. Impossible to prevent from happening
11. Harsh
12. Feeling of hopelessness or disappointment
13. Became thick or solid
14. Overturned; caused a boat to overturn
15. Stiff; stretched tight
16. Tool for cutting heavy pieces of wood

A=15	B=6	C=9	D=4
E=12	F=1	G=14	H=7
I=2	J=11	K=8	L=13
M=5	N=16	O=3	P=10

Call It Courage Vocabulary Magic Squares 3

Match the definition with the vocabulary word. Put your answers in the magic squares below. When your answers are correct, all columns and rows will add to the same number.

A. PERIL   E. ELATION   I. RELISHING   M. SEIZE
B. MUTTER   F. CAUTION   J. OPPRESSIVE   N. WROUGHT
C. LUMINOUS   G. SCORN   K. CAPSIZED   O. EXERTION
D. DISMAY   H. CONVULSIVELY   L. FIERCE   P. MISSIONARIES

1. Giving off or reflecting light
2. Harsh
3. Care; close attention
4. Physical effort
5. People sent by a church to spread its faith
6. Feeling of extraordinary happiness and excitement
7. Taking great pleasure in
8. Feeling of hopelessness or disappointment
9. Take hold of quickly and firmly
10. In a violently jerking or shaking manner
11. Ferocious; violent
12. Danger
13. Complain quietly or indistinctly
14. Overturned; caused a boat to overturn
15. Contempt; disrespect
16. Formed; created

A= 12	B= 13	C= 1	D= 8
E= 6	F= 3	G= 15	H= 10
I= 7	J= 2	K= 14	L= 11
M= 9	N= 16	O= 4	P= 5

Call It Courage Vocabulary Magic Squares 3 Answer Key

Match the definition with the vocabulary word. Put your answers in the magic squares below. When your answers are correct, all columns and rows will add to the same number.

A. PERIL
B. MUTTER
C. LUMINOUS
D. DISMAY
E. ELATION
F. CAUTION
G. SCORN
H. CONVULSIVELY
I. RELISHING
J. OPPRESSIVE
K. CAPSIZED
L. FIERCE
M. SEIZE
N. WROUGHT
O. EXERTION
P. MISSIONARIES

1. Giving off or reflecting light
2. Harsh
3. Care; close attention
4. Physical effort
5. People sent by a church to spread its faith
6. Feeling of extraordinary happiness and excitement
7. Taking great pleasure in
8. Feeling of hopelessness or disappointment
9. Take hold of quickly and firmly
10. In a violently jerking or shaking manner
11. Ferocious; violent
12. Danger
13. Complain quietly or indistinctly
14. Overturned; caused a boat to overturn
15. Contempt; disrespect
16. Formed; created

A=12	B=13	C=1	D=8
E=6	F=3	G=15	H=10
I=7	J=2	K=14	L=11
M=9	N=16	O=4	P=5

Call It Courage Vocabulary Magic Squares 4

Match the definition with the vocabulary word. Put your answers in the magic squares below. When your answers are correct, all columns and rows will add to the same number.

A. RELISHING   E. LASH   I. INEVITABLE   M. WANED
B. MISSIONARIES   F. INDIFFERENCE   J. LUMINOUS   N. IRRESOLUTE
C. BOLSTER   G. CONVULSIVELY   K. VANTAGE   O. ELATION
D. EXERTION   H. APPREHENSION   L. WROUGHT   P. DISMAL

1. Feeling of extraordinary happiness and excitement
2. Physical effort
3. Giving off or reflecting light
4. Tie something to another object
5. Impossible to prevent from happening
6. Lack of interest or concern
7. Depressing
8. Strengthen by encouraging
9. Worry; nervousness
10. Position that gives an advantage
11. Taking great pleasure in
12. Unsure; not able to make decisions
13. People sent by a church to spread its faith
14. Decreased; got smaller
15. In a violently jerking or shaking manner
16. Formed; created

A=	B=	C=	D=
E=	F=	G=	H=
I=	J=	K=	L=
M=	N=	O=	P=

Call It Courage Vocabulary Magic Squares 4 Answer Key

Match the definition with the vocabulary word. Put your answers in the magic squares below. When your answers are correct, all columns and rows will add to the same number.

A. RELISHING
B. MISSIONARIES
C. BOLSTER
D. EXERTION
E. LASH
F. INDIFFERENCE
G. CONVULSIVELY
H. APPREHENSION
I. INEVITABLE
J. LUMINOUS
K. VANTAGE
L. WROUGHT
M. WANED
N. IRRESOLUTE
O. ELATION
P. DISMAL

1. Feeling of extraordinary happiness and excitement
2. Physical effort
3. Giving off or reflecting light
4. Tie something to another object
5. Impossible to prevent from happening
6. Lack of interest or concern
7. Depressing
8. Strengthen by encouraging
9. Worry; nervousness
10. Position that gives an advantage
11. Taking great pleasure in
12. Unsure; not able to make decisions
13. People sent by a church to spread its faith
14. Decreased; got smaller
15. In a violently jerking or shaking manner
16. Formed; created

A=11	B=13	C=8	D=2
E=4	F=6	G=15	H=9
I=5	J=3	K=10	L=16
M=14	N=12	O=1	P=7

Call It Courage Vocabulary Word Search 1

```
R A M P A R T S U L T R Y V C R W D P J
Z P I R R Y R S F I E A C A A E R E O L
H P S O F Q C I R L M E O N U N O S I C
S R S F L P E P I S T D N T T D U P S F
M E I A F R L S I A D I G A E I G A E G
Y H O N C U H D R I N S E G R N H I D J
X E N E C I W T M O K M A E I G T R W F
Q N A D N X S I I Q G A L I Z N T I M B
U S R G K O N T S R V L E N E W N N U J
A I I H R I A X O J Z W D T G D A G T V
I O E P S L S T J P V K A E E C P X T D
L N S H E L E T M B E J G R A C I L E R
I C I T Y S N F O S R R U V I M F R R D
N N A L Q X R C U U I L I A N L E E S T
G E D U R S C O R N T P Z L W E Y U L M
D S E M T K N B S U A L K S J A T N A L
J E Z U K I S M A B B M I Q N E N C S F
L I D T M L O T F G L M N V P V S E H V
G Z A U D V C N S H E M K M I T C M D H
Y E L E X E R T I O N N I P V D G R P F
```

Balanced; suspended (6)
Became thick or solid (9)
Becoming smaller (11)
Bizarre; gross (9)
Brave; sturdy (5)
Care; close attention (7)
Cautiously (6)
Complain quietly or indistinctly (6)
Contempt; disrespect (5)
Cut down (4)
Danger (5)
Decreased; got smaller (5)
Depressing (6)
Distances between things (9)
Feeling hopeless (10)
Feeling of extraordinary happiness and excitement (7)
Feeling of hopelessness or disappointment (6)
Ferocious; violent (6)
Formed; created (7)
Forward motion; movement (7)
Giving off or reflecting light (8)
Gracefully slender (7)
Increased; enlarged (5)

Lie flat (9)
Mocked by shouting or laughing (6)
Noisy uproar (6)
People sent by a church to spread its faith (12)
Physical effort (8)
Position that gives an advantage (7)
Real; true (9)
Rough; incomplete (4)
Seal a wound with something that burns (9)
Showed disrespect for gods or a religion (8)
Someone who is responsible for a misdeed (7)
Stiff; stretched tight (4)
Take hold of quickly and firmly (5)
Taking great pleasure in (9)
Tearing apart violently (7)
Tempted someone to go somewhere (5)
Tie something to another object (4)
Tool for cutting heavy pieces of wood (4)
Trembling or shrinking back with fear (8)
Very angry (5)
Very hot and damp (6)
Walls of a fort (8)
Worry; nervousness (12)

Call It Courage Vocabulary Word Search 1 Answer Key

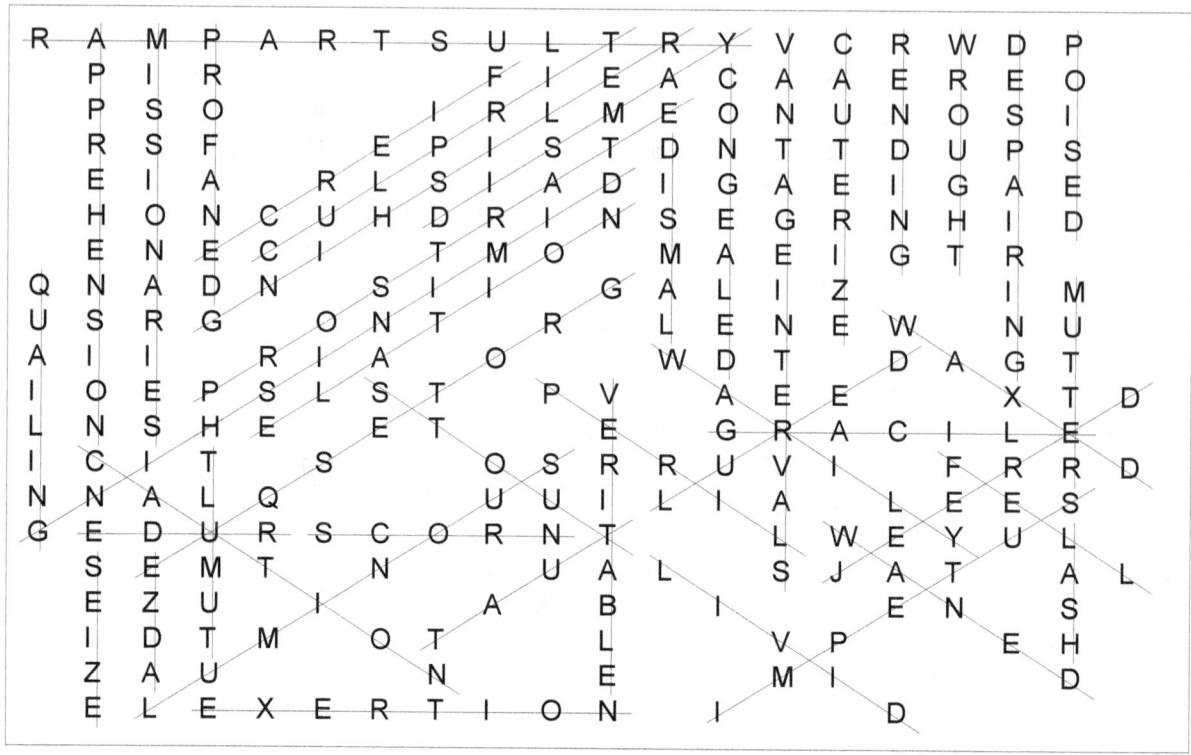

Balanced; suspended (6)
Became thick or solid (9)
Becoming smaller (11)
Bizarre; gross (9)
Brave; sturdy (5)
Care; close attention (7)
Cautiously (6)
Complain quietly or indistinctly (6)
Contempt; disrespect (5)
Cut down (4)
Danger (5)
Decreased; got smaller (5)
Depressing (6)
Distances between things (9)
Feeling hopeless (10)
Feeling of extraordinary happiness and excitement (7)
Feeling of hopelessness or disappointment (6)
Ferocious; violent (6)
Formed; created (7)
Forward motion; movement (7)
Giving off or reflecting light (8)
Gracefully slender (7)
Increased; enlarged (5)

Lie flat (9)
Mocked by shouting or laughing (6)
Noisy uproar (6)
People sent by a church to spread its faith (12)
Physical effort (8)
Position that gives an advantage (7)
Real; true (9)
Rough; incomplete (4)
Seal a wound with something that burns (9)
Showed disrespect for gods or a religion (8)
Someone who is responsible for a misdeed (7)
Stiff; stretched tight (4)
Take hold of quickly and firmly (5)
Taking great pleasure in (9)
Tearing apart violently (7)
Tempted someone to go somewhere (5)
Tie something to another object (4)
Tool for cutting heavy pieces of wood (4)
Trembling or shrinking back with fear (8)
Very angry (5)
Very hot and damp (6)
Walls of a fort (8)
Worry; nervousness (12)

Call It Courage Vocabulary Word Search 2

```
W A X E D E R E E J F E S C K Y V E C Q
L P R P E I N L L X P D A T A X C V O K
A I E E S V S W I X E U S M O R X I N G
S N N R I A E M C V T R S C E U R S G T
H N D I O N I P A E E I T I O E T S E W
F A I L P T Z G R L D R F I T R H E A S
N C N P Z A E I G E S M I S O D N R L C
B L G D I G Z M U G F S L T E N Y P E L
W E M F M E H Q F G T O B R A R X P D P
N T U I P H S J C R B S U L T B W O Y W
C N T M E E H W A A P L H L T T L Q K N
U H T P T K Q P A R P Z U L D I Q E R N
L G E O U C M Q O R S S U B Z M L D C W
P P R T S A D S U Y I M I V G P J E A M
R G U E R S T A H A U L F Z Q E B N U J
I A B N R R R D X T I P Y G E N E O T B
T A N T A L I Z I N G L I V I D W H I G
E L A T I O N E M C L L I J X I K P O S
B D E N A F O R P E H G N N Y N B I N X
W R O U G H T G F X G H L W G G M S X P
```

About to happen (9)
Balanced; suspended (6)
Became thick or solid (9)
Bizarre; gross (9)
Brave; sturdy (5)
Care; close attention (7)
Cautiously (6)
Complain quietly or indistinctly (6)
Contempt; disrespect (5)
Cut down (4)
Danger (5)
Decreased; got smaller (5)
Depressing (6)
Feeling of extraordinary happiness and excitement (7)
Feeling of hopelessness or disappointment (6)
Ferocious; violent (6)
Formed; created (7)
Forward motion; movement (7)
Gracefully slender (7)
Harsh (10)
Increased; enlarged (5)
Lie flat (9)
Mocked by shouting or laughing (6)

Noisy uproar (6)
Overturned; caused a boat to overturn (8)
Physical effort (8)
Position that gives an advantage (7)
Real; true (9)
Rough; incomplete (4)
Seal a wound with something that burns (9)
Showed disrespect for gods or a religion (8)
Someone who is responsible for a misdeed (7)
Stiff; stretched tight (4)
Strengthen by encouraging (7)
Take hold of quickly and firmly (5)
Tearing apart violently (7)
Tempted someone to go somewhere (5)
Tempting but unavailable (11)
Tie something to another object (4)
Tool for cutting heavy pieces of wood (4)
Top; highest point (8)
Transferred liquid through a tube (8)
Trembling or shrinking back with fear (8)
Very angry (5)
Very hot and damp (6)
Walls of a fort (8)
Without strength (8)

Call It Courage Vocabulary Word Search 2 Answer Key

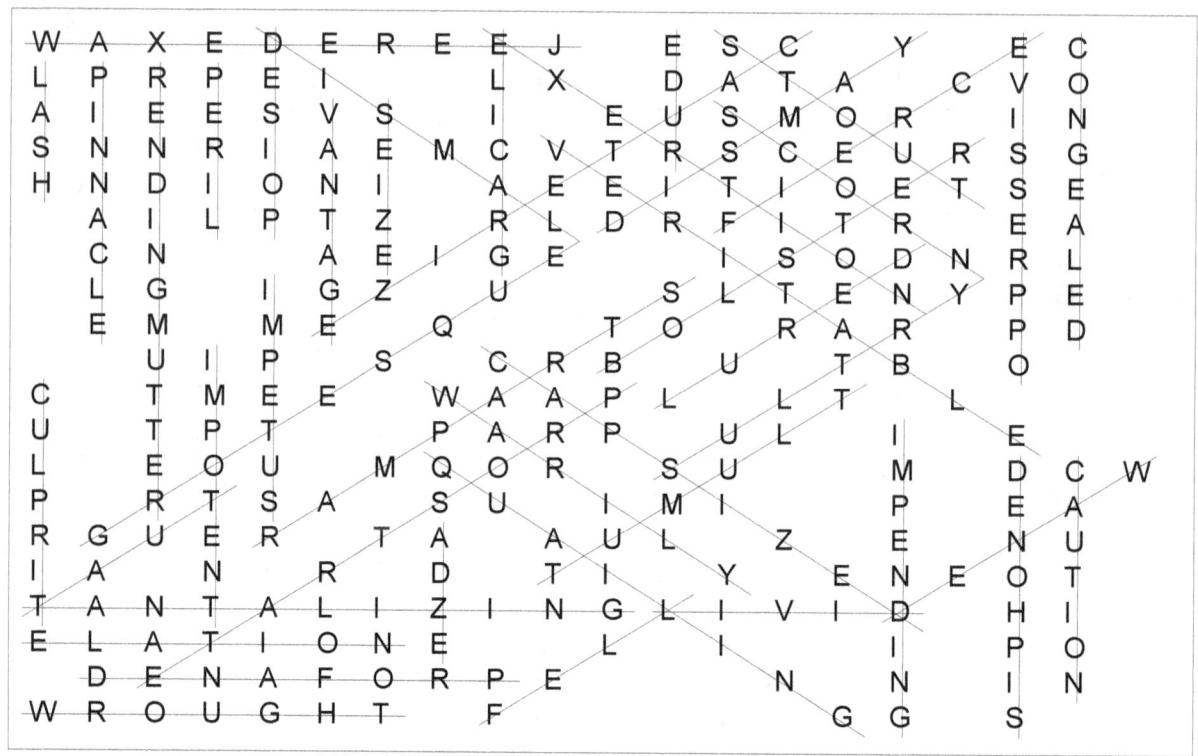

About to happen (9)
Balanced; suspended (6)
Became thick or solid (9)
Bizarre; gross (9)
Brave; sturdy (5)
Care; close attention (7)
Cautiously (6)
Complain quietly or indistinctly (6)
Contempt; disrespect (5)
Cut down (4)
Danger (5)
Decreased; got smaller (5)
Depressing (6)
Feeling of extraordinary happiness and excitement (7)
Feeling of hopelessness or disappointment (6)
Ferocious; violent (6)
Formed; created (7)
Forward motion; movement (7)
Gracefully slender (7)
Harsh (10)
Increased; enlarged (5)
Lie flat (9)
Mocked by shouting or laughing (6)

Noisy uproar (6)
Overturned; caused a boat to overturn (8)
Physical effort (8)
Position that gives an advantage (7)
Real; true (9)
Rough; incomplete (4)
Seal a wound with something that burns (9)
Showed disrespect for gods or a religion (8)
Someone who is responsible for a misdeed (7)
Stiff; stretched tight (4)
Strengthen by encouraging (7)
Take hold of quickly and firmly (5)
Tearing apart violently (7)
Tempted someone to go somewhere (5)
Tempting but unavailable (11)
Tie something to another object (4)
Tool for cutting heavy pieces of wood (4)
Top; highest point (8)
Transferred liquid through a tube (8)
Trembling or shrinking back with fear (8)
Very angry (5)
Very hot and damp (6)
Walls of a fort (8)
Without strength (8)

Call It Courage Vocabulary Word Search 3

```
I V S K W G W R Q T A N T A L I Z I N G
N F T Q Y A E K U S I W K C M C L R P
E D R K T T R K A O C M T C M P O L O H
V I A M T H G I I T J P S C H O N M C B
I M P U Q Z D D L S D E X A W T G I S Z
T I M G Q P E B I Y S N C P C E E N Z J
A N A E K R S F N P C D W S U N A O R L
B I R X E W P Y G H F I B I L T L U E Y
L S Z E N Z A T D V P N O Z P Z E S L Q
E H J R P M I Y E W A G L E R V D T I L
F I W T S D R T N S E N S D I S H T S V
Y N S I C E I R A I V T T P T G Z R H N
T G D O K R N Y F P I P E A U L X U I W
C B V N V U G W O H S R R O G L S D N T
G R A C I L E P R O S T R A T E P E G Z
K P P K N G I E P N E W V E I F L M V W
X O B L N R N V L E R J A R S B Q E Z S
G I A P O D T R I D P I A N A O Z B L S
W S S F I E R C E D P N M T E I L A S D
H E X N T N S S R L O V I P R D V U Y J
P D G T U Z N V U I A R N E E R T Y T Y
E W N N A N P A S L E T T V E T A G Z E
R G W B C P D S C V T U I T U M U L T Y
I S E I Z E I M F L A R N O J F T S K W
L X D I S M A L T C E I Y F N A D Z E K
```

ADZE	ELATION	JEERED	PROFANED	SULTRY
BOLSTER	EXERTION	LASH	PROSTRATE	TANTALIZING
CAPSIZED	FELL	LIVID	QUAILING	TAUT
CAUTERIZE	FIERCE	LUMINOUS	RAMPARTS	TUMULT
CAUTION	GRACILE	LURED	RELISHING	VANTAGE
CONGEALED	IMPENDING	MISSIONARIES	RENDING	VERITABLE
CULPRIT	IMPETUS	MUTTER	RUDE	WANED
DESPAIRING	IMPOTENT	OPPRESSIVE	SCORN	WARILY
DIMINISHING	INEVITABLE	PERIL	SEIZE	WAXED
DISMAL	INTERVALS	PINNACLE	SIPHONED	WROUGHT
DISMAY	IRRESOLUTE	POISED	STOUT	

Call It Courage Vocabulary Word Search 3 Answer Key

ADZE	ELATION	JEERED	PROFANED	SULTRY
BOLSTER	EXERTION	LASH	PROSTRATE	TANTALIZING
CAPSIZED	FELL	LIVID	QUAILING	TAUT
CAUTERIZE	FIERCE	LUMINOUS	RAMPARTS	TUMULT
CAUTION	GRACILE	LURED	RELISHING	VANTAGE
CONGEALED	IMPENDING	MISSIONARIES	RENDING	VERITABLE
CULPRIT	IMPETUS	MUTTER	RUDE	WANED
DESPAIRING	IMPOTENT	OPPRESSIVE	SCORN	WARILY
DIMINISHING	INEVITABLE	PERIL	SEIZE	WAXED
DISMAL	INTERVALS	PINNACLE	SIPHONED	WROUGHT
DISMAY	IRRESOLUTE	POISED	STOUT	

Call It Courage Vocabulary Word Search 4

ADZE	DISMAY	INTERVALS	POISED	STOUT
BOLSTER	ELATION	IRRESOLUTE	PROFANED	SULTRY
CAPSIZED	EXERTION	JEERED	PROSTRATE	TANTALIZING
CAUTERIZE	FELL	LASH	QUAILING	TAUT
CAUTION	FIERCE	LIVID	RAMPARTS	TUMULT
CONGEALED	GRACILE	LUMINOUS	RELISHING	VANTAGE
CONVULSIVELY	GROTESQUE	LURED	RENDING	VERITABLE
CULPRIT	IMPENDING	MISSIONARIES	RUDE	WANED
DESPAIRING	IMPETUS	MUTTER	SCORN	WARILY
DIMINISHING	IMPOTENT	PERIL	SEIZE	WAXED
DISMAL	INEVITABLE	PINNACLE	SIPHONED	WROUGHT

Call It Courage Vocabulary Word Search 4 Answer Key

ADZE	DISMAY	INTERVALS	POISED	STOUT
BOLSTER	ELATION	IRRESOLUTE	PROFANED	SULTRY
CAPSIZED	EXERTION	JEERED	PROSTRATE	TANTALIZING
CAUTERIZE	FELL	LASH	QUAILING	TAUT
CAUTION	FIERCE	LIVID	RAMPARTS	TUMULT
CONGEALED	GRACILE	LUMINOUS	RELISHING	VANTAGE
CONVULSIVELY	GROTESQUE	LURED	RENDING	VERITABLE
CULPRIT	IMPENDING	MISSIONARIES	RUDE	WANED
DESPAIRING	IMPETUS	MUTTER	SCORN	WARILY
DIMINISHING	IMPOTENT	PERIL	SEIZE	WAXED
DISMAL	INEVITABLE	PINNACLE	SIPHONED	WROUGHT

Call It Courage Vocabulary Crossword 1

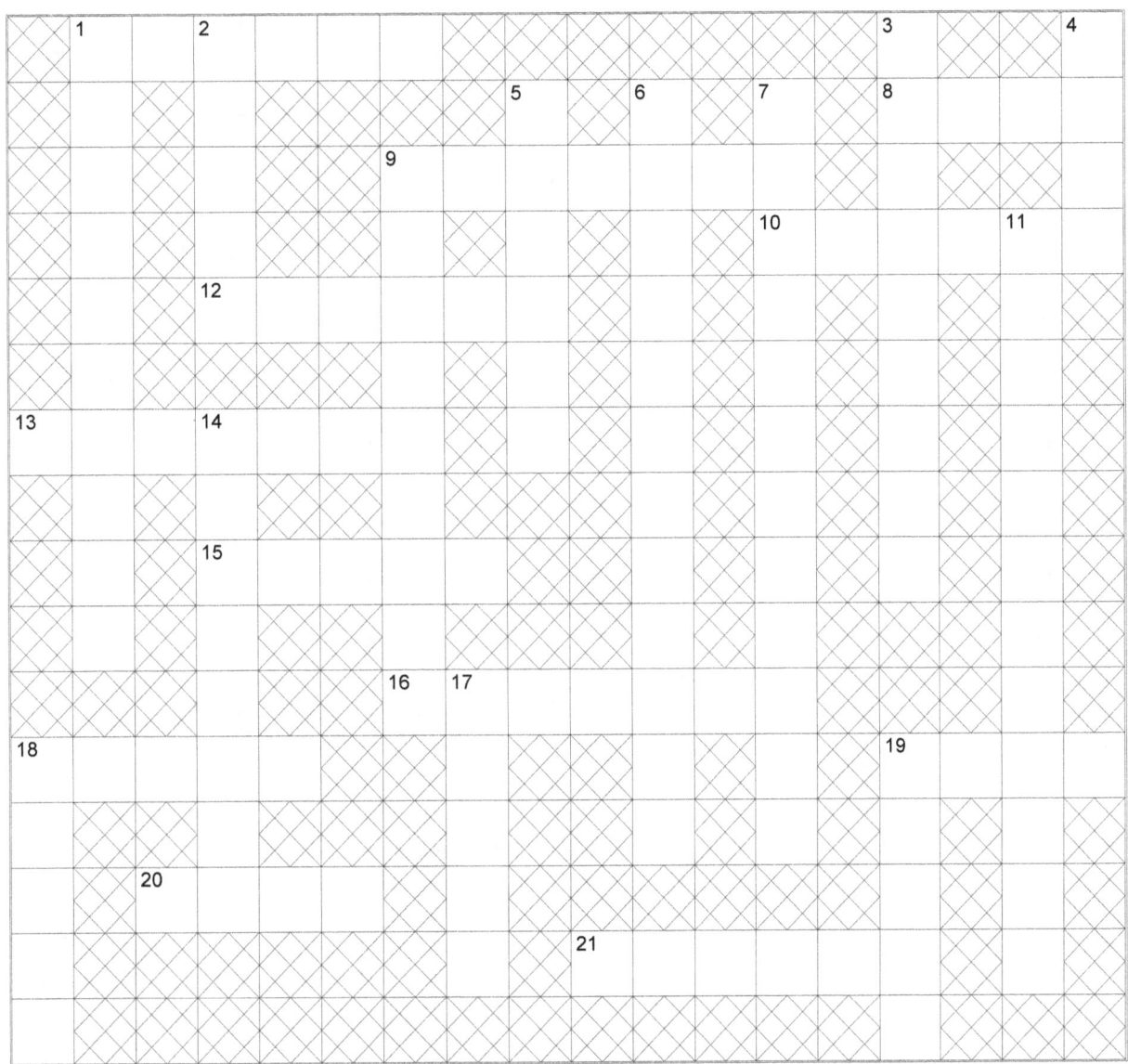

Across
1. Feeling of hopelessness or disappointment
8. Rough; incomplete
9. Care; close attention
10. Depressing
12. Noisy uproar
13. Gracefully slender
15. Danger
16. Feeling of extraordinary happiness and excitement
18. Take hold of quickly and firmly
19. Tie something to another object
20. Tool for cutting heavy pieces of wood
21. Ferocious; violent

Down
1. Feeling hopeless
2. Brave; sturdy
3. Lie flat
4. Cut down
5. Very hot and damp
6. People sent by a church to spread its faith
7. Lack of interest or concern
9. Seal a wound with something that burns
11. Worry; nervousness
14. Overturned; caused a boat to overturn
17. Very angry
18. Contempt; disrespect
19. Tempted someone to go somewhere

Call It Courage Vocabulary Crossword 1 Answer Key

Across
1. Feeling of hopelessness or disappointment
8. Rough; incomplete
9. Care; close attention
10. Depressing
12. Noisy uproar
13. Gracefully slender
15. Danger
16. Feeling of extraordinary happiness and excitement
18. Take hold of quickly and firmly
19. Tie something to another object
20. Tool for cutting heavy pieces of wood
21. Ferocious; violent

Down
1. Feeling hopeless
2. Brave; sturdy
3. Lie flat
4. Cut down
5. Very hot and damp
6. People sent by a church to spread its faith
7. Lack of interest or concern
9. Seal a wound with something that burns
11. Worry; nervousness
14. Overturned; caused a boat to overturn
17. Very angry
18. Contempt; disrespect
19. Tempted someone to go somewhere

Call It Courage Vocabulary Crossword 2

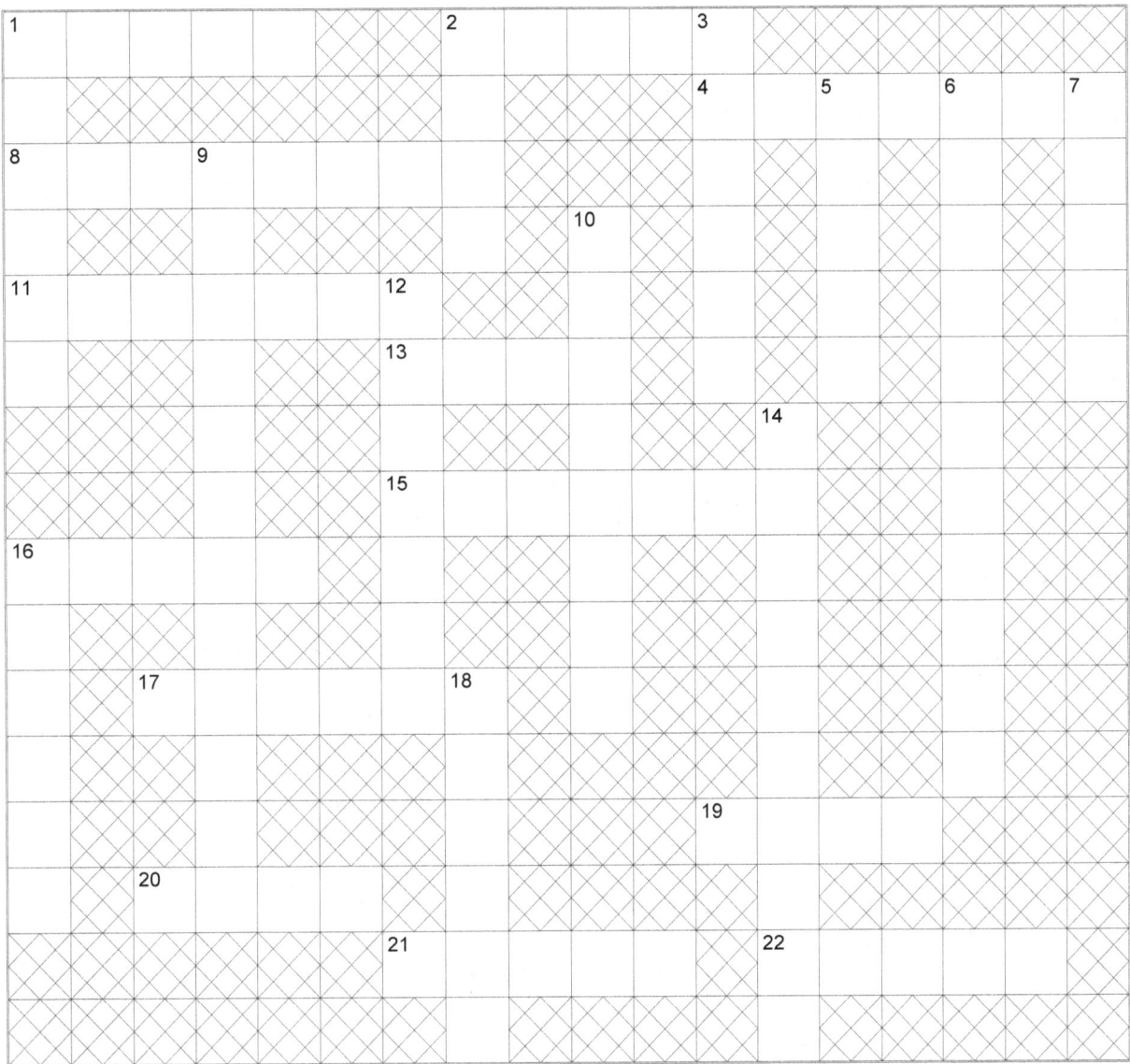

Across
1. Brave; sturdy
2. Very angry
4. Forward motion; movement
8. Giving off or reflecting light
11. Tearing apart violently
13. Rough; incomplete
15. Care; close attention
16. Increased; enlarged
17. Mocked by shouting or laughing
19. Stiff; stretched tight
20. Cut down
21. Decreased; got smaller
22. Tempted someone to go somewhere

Down
1. Very hot and damp
2. Tie something to another object
3. Depressing
5. Danger
6. Tempting but unavailable
7. Take hold of quickly and firmly
9. Lack of interest or concern
10. Physical effort
12. Gracefully slender
14. Impossible to prevent from happening
16. Cautiously
18. Feeling of hopelessness or disappointment

Call It Courage Vocabulary Crossword 2 Answer Key

	1 S	T	O	U	T		2 L	I	V	I	D	3 D			
	U						A				4 I	M	5 P	6 E	7 T	U	S
	8 L	U	9 M	I	N	O	U	S			S		E		A		E
	T		N				H		10 E		M		R		N		I
	11 R	E	N	D	I	12 N	G		X		A		I		T		Z
	Y		I			13 R	U	D	E		L		L		A		E
			F			A			R		14 I		L				
			F			15 C	A	U	T	I	O	N			I		
	16 W	A	X	E	D		I		I		N		E		Z		
	A		R				L		O				V		I		
	R		17 J	E	E	R	E	D	18 N				I		N		
	I		N				D						T		G		
	L		C				I				19 T	A	U	T			
	Y		20 F	E	L	L		S			A						
						21 W	A	N	E	D		22 L	U	R	E	D	
						Y					E						

Across
1. Brave; sturdy
2. Very angry
4. Forward motion; movement
8. Giving off or reflecting light
11. Tearing apart violently
13. Rough; incomplete
15. Care; close attention
16. Increased; enlarged
17. Mocked by shouting or laughing
19. Stiff; stretched tight
20. Cut down
21. Decreased; got smaller
22. Tempted someone to go somewhere

Down
1. Very hot and damp
2. Tie something to another object
3. Depressing
5. Danger
6. Tempting but unavailable
7. Take hold of quickly and firmly
9. Lack of interest or concern
10. Physical effort
12. Gracefully slender
14. Impossible to prevent from happening
16. Cautiously
18. Feeling of hopelessness or disappointment

Call It Courage Vocabulary Crossword 3

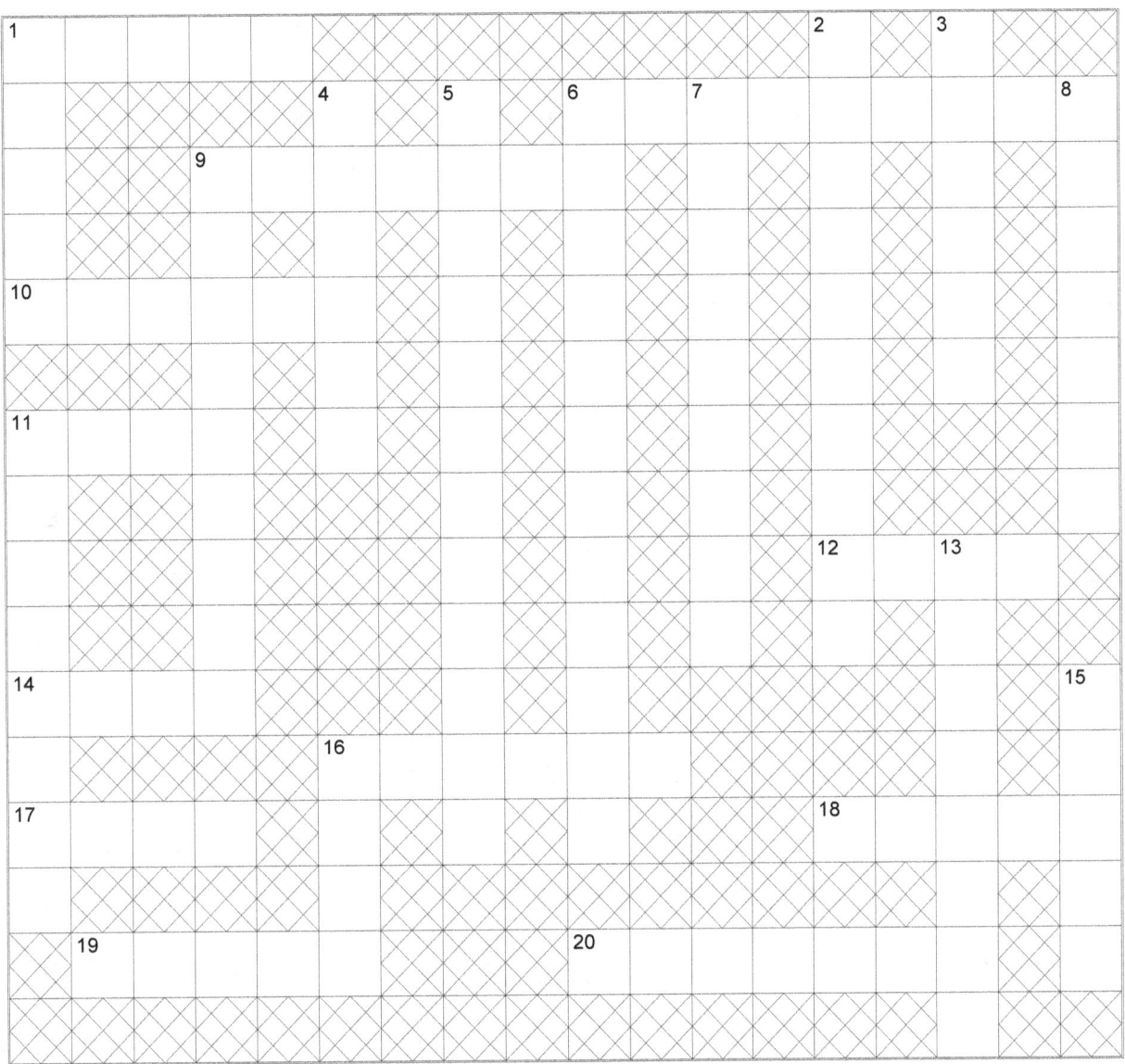

Across
1. Take hold of quickly and firmly
6. About to happen
9. Care; close attention
10. Noisy uproar
11. Rough; incomplete
12. Tie something to another object
14. Tool for cutting heavy pieces of wood
16. Ferocious; violent
17. Stiff; stretched tight
18. Contempt; disrespect
19. Danger
20. Position that gives an advantage

Down
1. Brave; sturdy
2. Impossible to prevent from happening
3. Depressing
4. Very hot and damp
5. People sent by a church to spread its faith
6. Lack of interest or concern
7. Lie flat
8. Gracefully slender
9. Seal a wound with something that burns
11. Walls of a fort
13. Transferred liquid through a tube
15. Decreased; got smaller
16. Cut down

Call It Courage Vocabulary Crossword 3 Answer Key

	1 S	E	I	Z	E						2 I		3 D		
	T				4 S		5 M		6 I	M	P	E	N	D	I	N	G
	O		9 C	A	U	T	I	O	N		R		E		S		R
	U		A		L		S		D		O		V		M		A
	10 T	U	M	U	L	T		S		I		S		I		A		C
			T		R		I		F		T		T		L		I
	11 R	U	D	E		Y		O		F		R		A				L
	A				R		N		E		A		B					E
	M				I		A		R		T		12 L	A	13 S	H	
	P				Z		R		E		E		E		I		
	14 A	D	Z	E			I		N						P		15 W
	R				16 F	I	E	R	C	E					H		A
	17 T	A	U	T		E		S		E				18 S	C	O	R	N
	S					L									N		E
			19 P	E	R	I	L			20 V	A	N	T	A	G	E		D

Across
1. Take hold of quickly and firmly
6. About to happen
9. Care; close attention
10. Noisy uproar
11. Rough; incomplete
12. Tie something to another object
14. Tool for cutting heavy pieces of wood
16. Ferocious; violent
17. Stiff; stretched tight
18. Contempt; disrespect
19. Danger
20. Position that gives an advantage

Down
1. Brave; sturdy
2. Impossible to prevent from happening
3. Depressing
4. Very hot and damp
5. People sent by a church to spread its faith
6. Lack of interest or concern
7. Lie flat
8. Gracefully slender
9. Seal a wound with something that burns
11. Walls of a fort
13. Transferred liquid through a tube
15. Decreased; got smaller
16. Cut down

Call It Courage Vocabulary Crossword 4

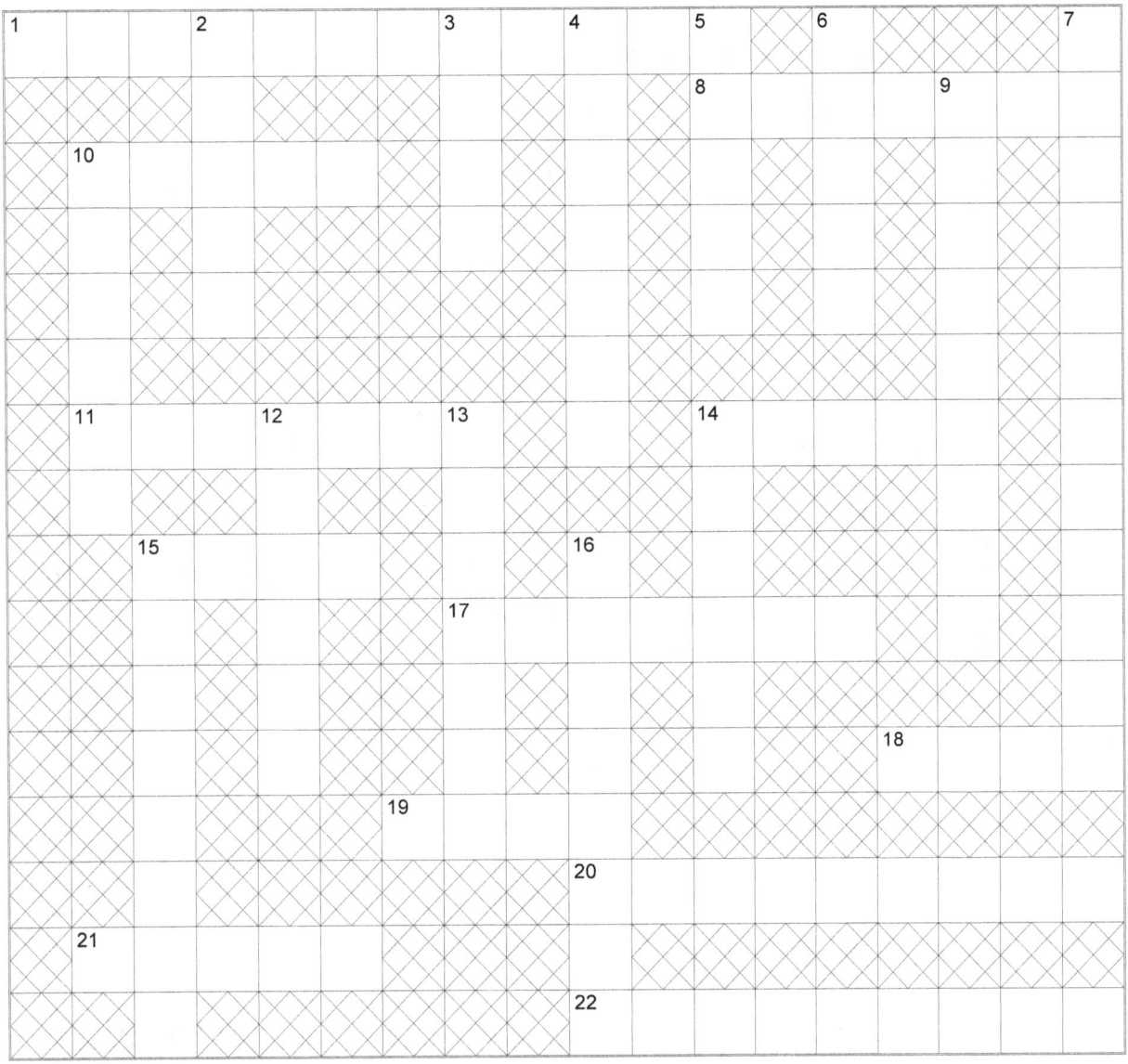

Across
1. People sent by a church to spread its faith
8. Feeling of extraordinary happiness and excitement
10. Brave; sturdy
11. Tearing apart violently
14. Decreased; got smaller
15. Tie something to another object
17. Care; close attention
18. Rough; incomplete
19. Cut down
20. Distances between things
21. Tempted someone to go somewhere
22. Bizarre; gross

Down
2. Contempt; disrespect
3. Tool for cutting heavy pieces of wood
4. Forward motion; movement
5. Take hold of quickly and firmly
6. Increased; enlarged
7. Lack of interest or concern
9. About to happen
10. Very hot and damp
12. Depressing
13. Gracefully slender
14. Cautiously
15. Giving off or reflecting light
16. Trembling or shrinking back with fear

Call It Courage Vocabulary Crossword 4 Answer Key

[Crossword grid with the following answers filled in:]

Across:
1. MISSIONARIES
8. ELATION
10. STOUT
11. RENDING
14. WANED
15. LASH
17. CAUTION
18. RUDE
19. FELL
20. INTERVALS
21. LURED
22. GROTESQUE

Down:
2. SCOURN (S-C-O-U-R-N... letters shown: S,C,O,U,L,T) — [grid shows: SCULT / column letters]
3. (column): TORN...
(Grid letters as shown in image)

Across
1. People sent by a church to spread its faith
8. Feeling of extraordinary happiness and excitement
10. Brave; sturdy
11. Tearing apart violently
14. Decreased; got smaller
15. Tie something to another object
17. Care; close attention
18. Rough; incomplete
19. Cut down
20. Distances between things
21. Tempted someone to go somewhere
22. Bizarre; gross

Down
2. Contempt; disrespect
3. Tool for cutting heavy pieces of wood
4. Forward motion; movement
5. Take hold of quickly and firmly
6. Increased; enlarged
7. Lack of interest or concern
9. About to happen
10. Very hot and damp
12. Depressing
13. Gracefully slender
14. Cautiously
15. Giving off or reflecting light
16. Trembling or shrinking back with fear

Call It Courage Vocabulary Juggle Review 1

1. ICGAERL = 1. _____
   Gracefully slender

2. TEPMISU = 2. _____
   Forward motion; movement

3. TVELEBAIR = 3. _____
   Real; true

4. PARSRATM = 4. _____
   Walls of a fort

5. LATNOIE = 5. _____
   Feeling of extraordinary happiness and excitement

6. EHDNSIOP = 6. _____
   Transferred liquid through a tube

7. LEBINVAEIT = 7. _____
   Impossible to prevent from happening

8. EOISNRASIISM = 8. _____
   People sent by a church to spread its faith

9. UTETMR = 9. _____
   Complain quietly or indistinctly

10. EOTNITMP =10. _____
    Without strength

11. YULRTS =11. _____
    Very hot and damp

12. GAINRIEDSP =12. _____
    Feeling hopeless

13. DIFFNEECRENI =13. _____
    Lack of interest or concern

14. VDIIL =14. _____
    Very angry

15. HIINMISIDGN =15. _____
    Becoming smaller

Call It Courage Vocabulary Juggle Review 1 Answer Key

1. ICGAERL = 1. GRACILE
   Gracefully slender
2. TEPMISU = 2. IMPETUS
   Forward motion; movement
3. TVELEBAIR = 3. VERITABLE
   Real; true
4. PARSRATM = 4. RAMPARTS
   Walls of a fort
5. LATNOIE = 5. ELATION
   Feeling of extraordinary happiness and excitement
6. EHDNSIOP = 6. SIPHONED
   Transferred liquid through a tube
7. LEBINVAEIT = 7. INEVITABLE
   Impossible to prevent from happening
8. EOISNRASIISM = 8. MISSIONARIES
   People sent by a church to spread its faith
9. UTETMR = 9. MUTTER
   Complain quietly or indistinctly
10. EOTNITMP =10. IMPOTENT
    Without strength
11. YULRTS =11. SULTRY
    Very hot and damp
12. GAINRIEDSP =12. DESPAIRING
    Feeling hopeless
13. DIFFNEECRENI =13. INDIFFERENCE
    Lack of interest or concern
14. VDIIL =14. LIVID
    Very angry
15. HIINMISIDGN =15. DIMINISHING
    Becoming smaller

Call It Courage Vocabulary Juggle Review 2

1. ITCLRPU = 1. _____
   Someone who is responsible for a misdeed

2. EEFICR = 2. _____
   Ferocious; violent

3. RDULE = 3. _____
   Tempted someone to go somewhere

4. HLAS = 4. _____
   Tie something to another object

5. UQAIGLIN = 5. _____
   Trembling or shrinking back with fear

6. OAERDNFP = 6. _____
   Showed disrespect for gods or a religion

7. RIMSIIEOASNS = 7. _____
   People sent by a church to spread its faith

8. SROCN = 8. _____
   Contempt; disrespect

9. DPSHNOIE = 9. _____
   Transferred liquid through a tube

10. MTUTLU = 10. _____
    Noisy uproar

11. SEYUNVVICLOL = 11. _____
    In a violently jerking or shaking manner

12. NMIDEGNPI = 12. _____
    About to happen

13. PREAROTST = 13. _____
    Lie flat

14. LTURYS = 14. _____
    Very hot and damp

15. LCNEPNAI = 15. _____
    Top; highest point

Call It Courage Vocabulary Juggle Review 2 Answer Key

1. ITCLRPU = 1. CULPRIT
   Someone who is responsible for a misdeed

2. EEFICR = 2. FIERCE
   Ferocious; violent

3. RDULE = 3. LURED
   Tempted someone to go somewhere

4. HLAS = 4. LASH
   Tie something to another object

5. UQAIGLIN = 5. QUAILING
   Trembling or shrinking back with fear

6. OAERDNFP = 6. PROFANED
   Showed disrespect for gods or a religion

7. RIMSIIEOASNS = 7. MISSIONARIES
   People sent by a church to spread its faith

8. SROCN = 8. SCORN
   Contempt; disrespect

9. DPSHNOIE = 9. SIPHONED
   Transferred liquid through a tube

10. MTUTLU = 10. TUMULT
    Noisy uproar

11. SEYUNVVICLOL = 11. CONVULSIVELY
    In a violently jerking or shaking manner

12. NMIDEGNPI = 12. IMPENDING
    About to happen

13. PREAROTST = 13. PROSTRATE
    Lie flat

14. LTURYS = 14. SULTRY
    Very hot and damp

15. LCNEPNAI = 15. PINNACLE
    Top; highest point

Call It Courage Vocabulary Juggle Review 3

1. ROLTBES = 1. _____
   Strengthen by encouraging

2. XNITEREO = 2. _____
   Physical effort

3. EURTMT = 3. _____
   Complain quietly or indistinctly

4. OAFPNDER = 4. _____
   Showed disrespect for gods or a religion

5. EGSNPDIRAI = 5. _____
   Feeling hopeless

6. IIINMIDGHSN = 6. _____
   Becoming smaller

7. IRIESNGLH = 7. _____
   Taking great pleasure in

8. TTUA = 8. _____
   Stiff; stretched tight

9. ACIEPNLN = 9. _____
   Top; highest point

10. LMTUTU =10. _____
    Noisy uproar

11. TOIENLA =11. _____
    Feeling of extraordinary happiness and excitement

12. RCLPUTI =12. _____
    Someone who is responsible for a misdeed

13. NIDIEEENRFCF =13. _____
    Lack of interest or concern

14. GDNCLEAEO =14. _____
    Became thick or solid

15. VIILD =15. _____
    Very angry

Call It Courage Vocabulary Juggle Review 3 Answer Key

1. ROLTBES = 1. BOLSTER
Strengthen by encouraging

2. XNITEREO = 2. EXERTION
Physical effort

3. EURTMT = 3. MUTTER
Complain quietly or indistinctly

4. OAFPNDER = 4. PROFANED
Showed disrespect for gods or a religion

5. EGSNPDIRAI = 5. DESPAIRING
Feeling hopeless

6. IIINMIDGHSN = 6. DIMINISHING
Becoming smaller

7. IRIESNGLH = 7. RELISHING
Taking great pleasure in

8. TTUA = 8. TAUT
Stiff; stretched tight

9. ACIEPNLN = 9. PINNACLE
Top; highest point

10. LMTUTU =10. TUMULT
Noisy uproar

11. TOIENLA =11. ELATION
Feeling of extraordinary happiness and excitement

12. RCLPUTI =12. CULPRIT
Someone who is responsible for a misdeed

13. NIDIEEENRFCF =13. INDIFFERENCE
Lack of interest or concern

14. GDNCLEAEO =14. CONGEALED
Became thick or solid

15. VIILD =15. LIVID
Very angry

Call It Courage Vocabulary Juggle Review 4

1. TRUACEEZI = 1. _____
   Seal a wound with something that burns

2. UIONLMUS = 2. _____
   Giving off or reflecting light

3. ATVEGAN = 3. _____
   Position that gives an advantage

4. PDGRSINIAE = 4. _____
   Feeling hopeless

5. RNEIPENOPAHS = 5. _____
   Worry; nervousness

6. OTWURGH = 6. _____
   Formed; created

7. ZLANNIAITTG = 7. _____
   Tempting but unavailable

8. LLEF = 8. _____
   Cut down

9. SOBTRLE = 9. _____
   Strengthen by encouraging

10. VCNOYUVILLES =10. _____
    In a violently jerking or shaking manner

11. NHSOPDIE =11. _____
    Transferred liquid through a tube

12. RWILAY =12. _____
    Cautiously

13. ENIALVTBEI =13. _____
    Impossible to prevent from happening

14. ERVIOSSEPP =14. _____
    Harsh

15. URTLYS =15. _____
    Very hot and damp

Call It Courage Vocabulary Juggle Review 4 Answer Key

1. TRUACEEZI = 1. CAUTERIZE
Seal a wound with something that burns

2. UIONLMUS = 2. LUMINOUS
Giving off or reflecting light

3. ATVEGAN = 3. VANTAGE
Position that gives an advantage

4. PDGRSINIAE = 4. DESPAIRING
Feeling hopeless

5. RNEIPENOPAHS = 5. APPREHENSION
Worry; nervousness

6. OTWURGH = 6. WROUGHT
Formed; created

7. ZLANNIAITTG = 7. TANTALIZING
Tempting but unavailable

8. LLEF = 8. FELL
Cut down

9. SOBTRLE = 9. BOLSTER
Strengthen by encouraging

10. VCNOYUVILLES = 10. CONVULSIVELY
In a violently jerking or shaking manner

11. NHSOPDIE = 11. SIPHONED
Transferred liquid through a tube

12. RWILAY = 12. WARILY
Cautiously

13. ENIALVTBEI = 13. INEVITABLE
Impossible to prevent from happening

14. ERVIOSSEPP = 14. OPPRESSIVE
Harsh

15. URTLYS = 15. SULTRY
Very hot and damp

ADZE	Tool for cutting heavy pieces of wood
APPREHENSION	Worry; nervousness
BOLSTER	Strengthen by encouraging
CAPSIZED	Overturned; caused a boat to overturn
CAUTERIZE	Seal a wound with something that burns

CAUTION	Care; close attention
CONGEALED	Became thick or solid
CONVULSIVELY	In a violently jerking or shaking manner
CULPRIT	Someone who is responsible for a misdeed
DESPAIRING	Feeling hopeless

DIMINISHING	Becoming smaller
DISMAL	Depressing
DISMAY	Feeling of hopelessness or disappointment
ELATION	Feeling of extraordinary happiness and excitement
EXERTION	Physical effort

FELL	Cut down
FIERCE	Ferocious; violent
GRACILE	Gracefully slender
GROTESQUE	Bizarre; gross
IMPENDING	About to happen

IMPETUS	Forward motion; movement
IMPOTENT	Without strength
INDIFFERENCE	Lack of interest or concern
INEVITABLE	Impossible to prevent from happening
INTERVALS	Distances between things

IRRESOLUTE	Unsure; not able to make decisions
JEERED	Mocked by shouting or laughing
LASH	Tie something to another object
LIVID	Very angry
LUMINOUS	Giving off or reflecting light

LURED	Tempted someone to go somewhere
MISSIONARIES	People sent by a church to spread its faith
MUTTER	Complain quietly or indistinctly
OPPRESSIVE	Harsh
PERIL	Danger

PINNACLE	Top; highest point
POISED	Balanced; suspended
PROFANED	Showed disrespect for gods or a religion
PROSTRATE	Lie flat
QUAILING	Trembling or shrinking back with fear

RAMPARTS	Walls of a fort
RELISHING	Taking great pleasure in
RENDING	Tearing apart violently
RUDE	Rough; incomplete
SCORN	Contempt; disrespect

SEIZE	Take hold of quickly and firmly
SIPHONED	Transferred liquid through a tube
STOUT	Brave; sturdy
SULTRY	Very hot and damp
TANTALIZING	Tempting but unavailable

TAUT	Stiff; stretched tight
TUMULT	Noisy uproar
VANTAGE	Position that gives an advantage
VERITABLE	Real; true
WANED	Decreased; got smaller

WARILY	Cautiously
WAXED	Increased; enlarged
WROUGHT	Formed; created

Call It Courage Vocabulary

WROUGHT	IMPETUS	JEERED	LURED	INDIFFERENCE
STOUT	TUMULT	MISSIONARIES	VANTAGE	SIPHONED
WAXED	EXERTION	FREE SPACE	PERIL	INTERVALS
ELATION	FIERCE	CAUTERIZE	DESPAIRING	TANTALIZING
INEVITABLE	CAUTION	DISMAL	WANED	PINNACLE

Call It Courage Vocabulary

LIVID	RENDING	FELL	APPREHENSION	DISMAY
TAUT	LUMINOUS	MUTTER	LASH	GROTESQUE
VERITABLE	IRRESOLUTE	FREE SPACE	QUAILING	POISED
BOLSTER	CULPRIT	SULTRY	ADZE	PROSTRATE
WARILY	SCORN	RELISHING	DIMINISHING	IMPENDING

Call It Courage Vocabulary

GROTESQUE	WANED	GRACILE	FIERCE	CONGEALED
ADZE	TUMULT	IMPETUS	RUDE	DESPAIRING
FELL	WAXED	FREE SPACE	MUTTER	PINNACLE
RENDING	PERIL	INEVITABLE	SCORN	CAUTION
TAUT	CAPSIZED	VANTAGE	QUAILING	RAMPARTS

Call It Courage Vocabulary

SULTRY	IMPENDING	IMPOTENT	POISED	INDIFFERENCE
CULPRIT	DIMINISHING	LURED	APPREHENSION	IRRESOLUTE
RELISHING	LASH	FREE SPACE	MISSIONARIES	STOUT
PROSTRATE	WARILY	OPPRESSIVE	DISMAL	BOLSTER
TANTALIZING	LUMINOUS	EXERTION	CAUTERIZE	DISMAY

Call It Courage Vocabulary

WANED	IRRESOLUTE	GRACILE	RUDE	CAPSIZED
MUTTER	LURED	PERIL	TAUT	SCORN
SULTRY	IMPOTENT	FREE SPACE	OPPRESSIVE	TUMULT
LASH	VANTAGE	IMPETUS	FELL	SIPHONED
POISED	WROUGHT	ADZE	DIMINISHING	CONVULSIVELY

Call It Courage Vocabulary

CULPRIT	FIERCE	PINNACLE	LIVID	TANTALIZING
RELISHING	CONGEALED	LUMINOUS	ELATION	MISSIONARIES
STOUT	INDIFFERENCE	FREE SPACE	GROTESQUE	CAUTERIZE
WAXED	SEIZE	WARILY	INTERVALS	QUAILING
DISMAY	DESPAIRING	CAUTION	JEERED	PROSTRATE

Call It Courage Vocabulary

FELL	ADZE	IMPOTENT	JEERED	RENDING
TUMULT	INEVITABLE	ELATION	IRRESOLUTE	SCORN
RAMPARTS	CAPSIZED	FREE SPACE	MISSIONARIES	PERIL
SEIZE	WAXED	FIERCE	WANED	LUMINOUS
SULTRY	CAUTERIZE	GROTESQUE	VANTAGE	LASH

Call It Courage Vocabulary

LURED	LIVID	IMPETUS	RUDE	CONGEALED
SIPHONED	DISMAL	POISED	OPPRESSIVE	CAUTION
GRACILE	DISMAY	FREE SPACE	WROUGHT	CONVULSIVELY
PINNACLE	APPREHENSION	DESPAIRING	DIMINISHING	INDIFFERENCE
PROSTRATE	QUAILING	TANTALIZING	CULPRIT	IMPENDING

Call It Courage Vocabulary

WAXED	FIERCE	ADZE	FELL	DIMINISHING
PROFANED	LUMINOUS	CAPSIZED	INDIFFERENCE	APPREHENSION
MUTTER	INEVITABLE	FREE SPACE	SEIZE	STOUT
BOLSTER	RELISHING	ELATION	IMPOTENT	WARILY
VANTAGE	SIPHONED	LURED	TUMULT	CULPRIT

Call It Courage Vocabulary

CAUTERIZE	SCORN	IRRESOLUTE	GRACILE	SULTRY
LASH	IMPETUS	PINNACLE	DISMAL	DESPAIRING
TANTALIZING	WROUGHT	FREE SPACE	MISSIONARIES	RAMPARTS
CAUTION	DISMAY	LIVID	OPPRESSIVE	EXERTION
TAUT	GROTESQUE	POISED	IMPENDING	PERIL

Call It Courage Vocabulary

ELATION	CAPSIZED	JEERED	WANED	INDIFFERENCE
VANTAGE	GRACILE	WAXED	IMPOTENT	MUTTER
CAUTERIZE	TANTALIZING	FREE SPACE	INEVITABLE	EXERTION
SEIZE	TAUT	LURED	DESPAIRING	PROFANED
RAMPARTS	STOUT	APPREHENSION	WARILY	INTERVALS

Call It Courage Vocabulary

WROUGHT	CONVULSIVELY	PERIL	MISSIONARIES	OPPRESSIVE
QUAILING	PROSTRATE	IMPENDING	FIERCE	RELISHING
RUDE	DIMINISHING	FREE SPACE	VERITABLE	IMPETUS
LIVID	SCORN	CONGEALED	BOLSTER	FELL
TUMULT	CULPRIT	IRRESOLUTE	LUMINOUS	DISMAL

Call It Courage Vocabulary

SULTRY	CONVULSIVELY	CULPRIT	ELATION	DESPAIRING
LURED	PERIL	CAPSIZED	PINNACLE	WAXED
LUMINOUS	SIPHONED	FREE SPACE	LIVID	WARILY
OPPRESSIVE	IMPENDING	MISSIONARIES	FIERCE	IMPETUS
VANTAGE	DISMAL	TANTALIZING	RENDING	PROFANED

Call It Courage Vocabulary

POISED	GROTESQUE	FELL	IRRESOLUTE	APPREHENSION
LASH	IMPOTENT	TUMULT	ADZE	RELISHING
CONGEALED	BOLSTER	FREE SPACE	CAUTION	SCORN
DISMAY	TAUT	DIMINISHING	WANED	INEVITABLE
RAMPARTS	GRACILE	WROUGHT	INTERVALS	STOUT

Call It Courage Vocabulary

ELATION	SULTRY	EXERTION	LASH	SIPHONED
JEERED	WAXED	POISED	CAPSIZED	IRRESOLUTE
IMPENDING	IMPETUS	FREE SPACE	ADZE	CAUTION
LURED	CONGEALED	GROTESQUE	PINNACLE	TUMULT
MUTTER	GRACILE	RAMPARTS	CULPRIT	SEIZE

Call It Courage Vocabulary

TANTALIZING	DISMAY	STOUT	INDIFFERENCE	VERITABLE
TAUT	DIMINISHING	FELL	LIVID	INEVITABLE
FIERCE	BOLSTER	FREE SPACE	MISSIONARIES	APPREHENSION
DESPAIRING	RUDE	PERIL	CAUTERIZE	IMPOTENT
QUAILING	SCORN	WROUGHT	LUMINOUS	INTERVALS

Call It Courage Vocabulary

IRRESOLUTE	RENDING	SULTRY	WROUGHT	TUMULT
APPREHENSION	SEIZE	CONVULSIVELY	POISED	INDIFFERENCE
LIVID	IMPOTENT	FREE SPACE	LUMINOUS	DISMAY
PROSTRATE	FELL	CULPRIT	EXERTION	CAUTERIZE
RUDE	WAXED	DIMINISHING	VANTAGE	WANED

Call It Courage Vocabulary

STOUT	JEERED	TAUT	IMPETUS	TANTALIZING
MISSIONARIES	ADZE	QUAILING	DISMAL	ELATION
MUTTER	WARILY	FREE SPACE	CAPSIZED	SCORN
CONGEALED	DESPAIRING	CAUTION	PINNACLE	LASH
PERIL	INEVITABLE	GROTESQUE	VERITABLE	LURED

Call It Courage Vocabulary

RELISHING	DISMAL	PROSTRATE	APPREHENSION	ADZE
QUAILING	CONGEALED	IRRESOLUTE	MUTTER	GRACILE
TAUT	PERIL	FREE SPACE	JEERED	LURED
IMPENDING	CAUTION	FELL	MISSIONARIES	SIPHONED
BOLSTER	LIVID	GROTESQUE	PROFANED	DESPAIRING

Call It Courage Vocabulary

SEIZE	RENDING	WROUGHT	IMPOTENT	INEVITABLE
LASH	INTERVALS	IMPETUS	WARILY	FIERCE
POISED	STOUT	FREE SPACE	VANTAGE	INDIFFERENCE
WAXED	CAPSIZED	PINNACLE	LUMINOUS	ELATION
CAUTERIZE	OPPRESSIVE	CULPRIT	DIMINISHING	SULTRY

Call It Courage Vocabulary

DIMINISHING	IMPENDING	CULPRIT	INTERVALS	RENDING
TUMULT	TAUT	CAUTION	JEERED	LIVID
SIPHONED	IRRESOLUTE	FREE SPACE	RAMPARTS	LUMINOUS
DISMAY	FIERCE	PERIL	SEIZE	ELATION
EXERTION	STOUT	DISMAL	SULTRY	CAUTERIZE

Call It Courage Vocabulary

INDIFFERENCE	FELL	RELISHING	CONGEALED	CONVULSIVELY
WAXED	GRACILE	DESPAIRING	ADZE	RUDE
BOLSTER	VERITABLE	FREE SPACE	LASH	WARILY
GROTESQUE	OPPRESSIVE	SCORN	PINNACLE	QUAILING
LURED	WANED	CAPSIZED	WROUGHT	APPREHENSION

Call It Courage Vocabulary

VANTAGE	TAUT	MUTTER	PERIL	INDIFFERENCE
SULTRY	WROUGHT	DISMAY	PROSTRATE	IMPOTENT
RENDING	APPREHENSION	FREE SPACE	WAXED	OPPRESSIVE
ELATION	STOUT	CAUTERIZE	WANED	VERITABLE
SIPHONED	LIVID	CONGEALED	JEERED	GRACILE

Call It Courage Vocabulary

SCORN	PINNACLE	IMPENDING	CAPSIZED	QUAILING
RUDE	RELISHING	TANTALIZING	LUMINOUS	WARILY
PROFANED	FELL	FREE SPACE	DESPAIRING	CULPRIT
SEIZE	EXERTION	IMPETUS	MISSIONARIES	DIMINISHING
LASH	INTERVALS	IRRESOLUTE	RAMPARTS	ADZE

Call It Courage Vocabulary

FELL	GROTESQUE	CAPSIZED	RAMPARTS	SCORN
RENDING	SEIZE	CULPRIT	DESPAIRING	LIVID
CAUTERIZE	ELATION	FREE SPACE	PINNACLE	PERIL
PROFANED	VANTAGE	SULTRY	LURED	WARILY
RELISHING	POISED	QUAILING	TUMULT	WANED

Call It Courage Vocabulary

RUDE	IMPETUS	PROSTRATE	CONGEALED	DISMAY
WAXED	IMPOTENT	STOUT	CONVULSIVELY	INDIFFERENCE
ADZE	BOLSTER	FREE SPACE	VERITABLE	SIPHONED
LUMINOUS	MISSIONARIES	IMPENDING	OPPRESSIVE	WROUGHT
TANTALIZING	JEERED	IRRESOLUTE	GRACILE	DIMINISHING

Call It Courage Vocabulary

EXERTION	CONVULSIVELY	CULPRIT	ELATION	WAXED
OPPRESSIVE	WANED	STOUT	MISSIONARIES	SEIZE
IMPETUS	PINNACLE	FREE SPACE	JEERED	GRACILE
RELISHING	ADZE	FELL	TANTALIZING	POISED
PROFANED	CONGEALED	DESPAIRING	CAUTERIZE	APPREHENSION

Call It Courage Vocabulary

VANTAGE	PROSTRATE	PERIL	VERITABLE	CAPSIZED
WARILY	IRRESOLUTE	WROUGHT	IMPOTENT	INDIFFERENCE
IMPENDING	SULTRY	FREE SPACE	TUMULT	TAUT
RENDING	QUAILING	MUTTER	LURED	INEVITABLE
LASH	SIPHONED	DIMINISHING	LUMINOUS	GROTESQUE

Call It Courage Vocabulary

WAXED	TUMULT	LURED	RUDE	ADZE
ELATION	CAUTERIZE	LASH	IRRESOLUTE	INTERVALS
GRACILE	FIERCE	FREE SPACE	LIVID	IMPOTENT
IMPENDING	DIMINISHING	FELL	DESPAIRING	QUAILING
CONGEALED	IMPETUS	DISMAL	PINNACLE	BOLSTER

Call It Courage Vocabulary

STOUT	OPPRESSIVE	JEERED	LUMINOUS	RELISHING
VANTAGE	WANED	VERITABLE	TANTALIZING	CONVULSIVELY
CAPSIZED	PROSTRATE	FREE SPACE	RAMPARTS	DISMAY
INDIFFERENCE	EXERTION	MUTTER	RENDING	SIPHONED
SCORN	PROFANED	SEIZE	WROUGHT	GROTESQUE

Call It Courage Vocabulary

IMPENDING	WARILY	GRACILE	INTERVALS	PINNACLE
DESPAIRING	DIMINISHING	DISMAY	EXERTION	PERIL
FELL	BOLSTER	FREE SPACE	JEERED	POISED
MISSIONARIES	VERITABLE	CAUTERIZE	RAMPARTS	VANTAGE
TUMULT	SEIZE	FIERCE	ADZE	OPPRESSIVE

Call It Courage Vocabulary

CONGEALED	TANTALIZING	CONVULSIVELY	WANED	CAPSIZED
IMPETUS	INEVITABLE	SULTRY	WROUGHT	RENDING
CULPRIT	WAXED	FREE SPACE	RUDE	PROFANED
LUMINOUS	RELISHING	DISMAL	STOUT	LURED
LASH	ELATION	CAUTION	INDIFFERENCE	MUTTER